The Prosperity Secret

Success in the New World

by Markus Rothkranz

Contents

We are on the verge of a new world.

Many people are scared.

You might think it frivolous to have a book on prosperity

when world economies are collapsing.

Now is actually the most crucial time for you to do so

because you represent the new conscious world of good.

It is your DUTY to become powerful, so people

like you can stand strong and do things differently this time.

The richest people become rich during hard times

because change is opportunity.

You are the new world.

A world where everyone prospers.

Markus

Introduction

It's when you have nothing that you can do anything.
Things have been taken away from you because they were
holding you back. When you have nothing left to lose, you
have no more fear. When you are fearless, you are unstoppable.
You've been crawling like a caterpillar. It's time to break out of
your cocoon and spread your wings to fly above the problems.

When I gave up everything and had my 40 days, I was naked in
the desert with nothing, I mean NOTHING! Not even clothing.
When I came back to society, I lived in a friends closet for
several weeks. I was literally living in someone's closet. Within
90 days I was driving a Ferrari. Two months later, I also had
two Lotus turbo Esprits and a Mercedes convertible. I had no
more health problems. My clothing was custom made thousand
dollar outfits. I flew first class around the world. I hung out with
famous rock bands and I wrote and directed my own 2.5 million
dollar film which played in theaters all over the world. I don't
answer to anyone and I am free to do anything I want, anytime,
any place.

I don't need those fancy things now to be happy, but it's nice to
know I can get them whenever I want. That's freedom!

What's really important here is that the economy, talent, skill,
hard work, luck and who I know has <u>nothing</u> to do with it.

If you go after money, you'll only push it away. It needs to
come to you.

I hate to say this, but no one is going to help you with your money problems.

Except YOU.

This is a big lesson for most, and the moment you realize that the person you have been waiting for is YOU, the sooner you get on with your life. What you really want is freedom- right? Well the Universe gave you total freedom... no interference. Since no one is going to help you, you must do it yourself.

If you constantly depend on other people to keep you going and pay your bills at the last minute, then you're probably getting more stressed and worried as the economy becomes more unstable and people all around are losing everything.

When life takes away your house, your job, your car and your dysfunctional relationships, it's taking a great load of burden off your shoulders, whether it is forcefully taken against your will, or, you just give it all up like I did... what you are doing is being simplified down to your core being- THE REAL YOU. When you have nothing left is when you are the most free. There is nothing stopping you now, nothing is holding you back.

The most powerful warrior is the one who has nothing to lose.

"Strike me down, and I will be more powerful than you could ever imagine"

Obiwan Kenobi- Star Wars

Who am I ?

Many people think I am rich and famous because I have lots of talent. Unfortunately that's not what did it. As a matter of fact, all my talents did was slow me down. Others think because I worked in Hollywood, it must be from the connections I had. Sadly, that's not true either. What a waste of time those big-talking people were. All they did was say nice things and string me along.

What ultimately got me 2.5 million dollars to make my first motion picture was not talent, who I knew, my looks, luck or anything else you might suspect. It took me thirty years to figure it out, and when it dawned on me, it hit me in less than a minute. It was a flash that changed my life and opened my eyes to something so elegant and powerful, it forever changed the way I looked at things.

Then I looked at other successful people and noticed they had the same qualities. They weren't particularly talented in any way, or good looking or magical. They were normal people. I have been around rich and famous people all my life and I always wondered what made them different. It was like some unspoken secret they kept to themselves. It wasn't until I experienced the awakening myself that I realized they really weren't hiding anything from us. There was no conspiracy where the rich kept their secrets from us normal people to keep us poor so they can get richer. Stop listening to the fear-mongers. I am doing better now than I ever have in my life.

Nothing's been hidden from us. It's not a "SECRET". There is no brotherhood "code" shared only among exclusive members.

Anyone trying to sell you that crap is just trying to make a buck off you. It doesn't matter if there is a giant government conspiracy or not. The truth will set you free. Nothing can stop it. All it takes is not putting any more energy into fear and doing what you are here to do.

The answer has been with you all along. Not in front of you, but inside you. The rich and famous have actually openly shared this information with us, but we just weren't ready to receive and accept it. Not because it was too complicated, but because it was too simple.

The truth is so simple, a child or animal can instantly understand it. Why? Because they don't think too much. Our stupid thoughts get in the way and sabotage most of our greatest moments in life.

Be ready for anything, because success can hit you in the face unexpectedly fast and hard. Often times it's not where you expect it to come from.

It wasn't my photorealistic paintings or my work in the motion picture business that made me famous. You'll laugh.

What we consider unwanted "bad" things in our lives are usually our greatest gifts if we allow them to be.

You see, I was born with a weak immune system and almost died four times in my life. I had no idea what real health was. To this day, I never drank a drop of alcohol, smoked a cigarette or did any recreational drugs. Yet by the time I was 28, I was dying. My heart was collapsing, my liver was clogged, my kidneys were shot and I was bleeding when I went to the bathroom. I was unhappy with my life, making no money, my relationship was strained and oh yeah, I was dying. I looked around sadly and saw the whole world having one big party. Everyone else was having more fun, more sex, traveling the world, becoming famous, doing great things, and me... I had all this talent, nobody knew who I was, I had no money and I was dying. What was I missing? What was I doing wrong? I was thinking the very same thoughts you are probably running through your head right now.

Motivation will almost always beat mere talent. – Norman R. Augustine

First, let's make a distinction between rich and famous. Being famous does not necessarily mean rich (and vise versa). Actually most really really, rich people are off the radar. You've never heard of them and they like it that way.

I worked in Hollywood for twenty years for some of the biggest directors, producers and actors like Steven Spielberg, George Lucas, Aaron Spelling, Arnold Schwarzenegger, and many more. I sold my house to the drummer of the rock band Guns N' Roses and worked with guitarist Slash to create and produce the Guns N' Roses pinball machine with Sega Pinball out of Chicago. I became the world's top pinball artist and did merchandising, design work and special effects for blockbuster movies like Total Recall, Lethal Weapon, Jurassic Park, Star Wars etc. Money flowed, but most people didn't know who I was. I was flown in private jets and hung out with the biggest rock bands in Hollywood. This is not what I call "rich" though.

I was not healthy and it wasn't because of drugs, alcohol or cigarettes, I never touched those. No. I was dying because I was living the normal American lifestyle- eating bread, pasta, cereal, milk, sugar, pastries, cheese, and all kinds of cooked, processed crap you would never find in nature.

It took me 30 years to figure out what real health and prosperity was, (prosperity is a form of health) and it wasn't until I gave up everything, went to the desert, took my clothes off and had my 40 days, that I realized how simple the truth really was. It was all around us all along. It doesn't cost anything and it can make us healthier and richer than we could ever imagine.

I realized we are the only species that cooks its food and the only species that gets degenerative diseases like heart disease, diabetes, colon, breast, prostate cancer etc. The only animals that get those diseases are the ones fed by man or eat garbage left over by man. So I stopped cooking my food and only ate things found in nature... meaning no more bread, pasta, cereal etc. ...and guess what? All my health problems went away. I didn't even need glasses anymore. I felt alive like never before.

So I made a little informative video called "Go Raw Now". It wasn't selling anything. It was just an inspirational message to share with others what I had discovered. It made me world famous practically overnight. If you go to Youtube and type in the words "raw food", it is the most watched video in the world on the subject. I actually became the forth most famous Markus on Google.

Then I wrote a book on the subject called "Heal Yourself 101". It hit Amazon top 30 within 2 weeks and sold out in Europe. I am now flown all over the world to speak in front of thousands, usually it's standing room only. I've met heads of government and have been flown to secret military bases as a health consultant. After I came out with a documentary called "FREE FOOD AND MEDICINE", I was asked by American Indian elders to come and speak to their people about living off the land. Can you believe this? Indians asking a white guy to show them how to live off the land??? What is the world coming to?

This totally proves how ungrounded this world has become. People have lost touch with the truth. They don't know what's natural and real anymore. Now the economy is collapsing.

I started seeing a correlation between health issues and money issues. I realized the reason most people aren't rich is for the exact same reason most people aren't healthy. 95% of people in the modern world aren't healthy and 95% of people aren't wealthy. This was an exciting discovery and I realized I was seriously on to something. That's why I wrote this book.

Financial health has the same formula as physical health. The truth is amazingly simple. It's universal in all categories.

But it's not all simply about money. Sure I was rich, but I wasn't happy or healthy or doing anything I consider of any real value. I was not in touch with my true calling, and I felt empty, like I was living a lie. It wasn't me. So, in my opinion, simply having money is not success.

Prosperity is an energy thing. It is a sharing of life and positive energy with others and the universe. It wasn't until I did that health video (with no expectations of getting anything in return), that everything changed. I wasn't just making money. Now I was actually making a difference in the world. I was helping others. And this time, the money flowed with positive energy. I enjoyed what I did. I was prosperous. I was finally me.

Forget the economy. After you read this book, it doesn't matter if the entire country collapses. Forget all that MLM crap or anything else where you have to rely on other people for your money or well being.

Contained within the word impossible

Is the word Possible

Markus Rothkranz

Your Prosperity Starts Now

Your life is about to change. Forever.

When you learn the secret of prosperity and success, it doesn't just affect money… it changes everything in your life. That is a good sign you are dealing with the truth, because everything is connected and works off the same principles.

This book is not just about making money. True prosperity is much more than that. It is the freedom to be yourself and do whatever you want. In this book, I will use the terms "Rich" and "Poor". This does not just pertain to money. "Rich" people in my book are people who are successful, happy and free. "Poor" people are unhappy with their lives, not where they want to be, and feel they don't have the freedom to do what they want.

The answer is so simple, it's <u>unbelievable</u> for most people.

Which is exactly why most people remain stuck in an unhappy rut of bills, fear and misery. Even if you threw them a rope, they wouldn't grab it because they don't believe it will really pull them out of their misery. Skepticism is one of the biggest success killers. Do you want to continue being one of those people? You may say no, but if you really mean it, you must be ready to let go of everything in your life you hold valuable. Are you ready to do that? I'll give you a moment to really think about that.

Notice I didn't say you <u>will</u> get rid of everything. You just must be ok with the thought of completely starting over in life. Don't worry - the things that are truly for your highest good will remain. But everything else must fall away. So yes, some of you might have to completely start over. Each person is different.

 I will be blunt and direct with you in this book because I don't waste time.

I want results and I know you do too. So let's just get right to it.

Erase Your Programming

On the outside you are saying you want lots of money, but on the inside, I'll bet it's a different story. If you are carrying messed up conflicting emotions on the subject of money, emotions (the subconscious) will always win over logic (what you say on the outside).

If money seems to constantly fall away leaving you with little or nothing, then you have faulty energy programming.

I will explain this better later on, but what you think is YOU is actually a collection of everything you have absorbed from the moment you were conceived. You absorbed the thoughts, feelings, emotions and beliefs of your parents, of everything you've ever seen on TV, the news, the newspapers, magazines, movies, radio, songs, church, friends, teachers, strangers, coworkers, government, advertising and now the internet. You absorbed all the rumors, conspiracy theories, ideas and ramblings of everyone you ever heard speak and everything you've ever read. On the outside, you may believe or not believe something, but on the inside... your subconscious doesn't know the difference. The cells in your body only follow instructions from your control center (your head) which receives signals from the outside world (sight, sound, smell, taste). This all comes in through your head. For example, when you were a kid, some bully may have told you that you were ugly. Your brain says "no I'm not!" but that's just a knee-jerk reaction. Deep inside you have doubts "am I really ugly? Is this true?" This can stay with you your whole life and affect everything you do.

The same goes for money.

When you were a child, did your parents have money issues?
Did they work hard and make very little? At the end of the day,
was there no money left?

The fire of life is inside you
The fire of death is outside you.

The Essene Gospel of Peace

Lesson number one
Just because someone said it, doesn't make it so

Did you hear things like "Rich people are greedy dishonest bad people", "Money is the root of all evil", "Money turns good people bad", "That money could go to the poor", "The rich feed off the poor", "Rich people are the cause of our problems", "Rich people don't care- they are heartless", "Rich people screw people", "I never want to be like them", "Money doesn't grow on trees", "Money doesn't buy happiness", "There's only so much money to go around", "The rich get rich and the poor get poorer", "Money isn't that important", "People should only make enough to have a decent living", "There are people starving in India", "Not right now, we can't afford it, maybe someday", "Work hard for your money", "Men make money, women don't", "Men make more money than women", "Earn a decent living by working hard", "Get a real job", "Friday paycheck", "I wish money didn't exist", "Money, money, money. I'm tired of having to deal with money" "At least poor people have integrity" "Rich people are in with the government and all of them are corrupt, every one of them" "don't ever become one of those!". The list goes on. I could fill an entire book with the sound bytes we absorbed over our entire lifetime.

Any of this sound familiar?

How much of this did you hear as a child growing up? How much of it do you think you picked up through the womb while your parents were talking, preparing for your arrival and discussing what you would cost them financially.

How about this one *"no matter how hard I work, I always only seem to make just enough to pay the bills and there's never anything left"* (accompanied with a lot of frustration and pulling out of hair)

Let me guess. Thirty years later you are just making enough to pay the bills with not one penny left.

Hmmm. Now where did that come from?

Surely you had nothing to do with it, right? You are just a helpless victim of society. Everyone else is struggling, and so are you. People think worrying every month if the bills are going to be paid is normal. They think "barely making it" is normal. We look around and see most people living like this, so we accept this as normal and don't try to change.

Well those are the people you see. That doesn't mean there aren't just as many successful people out there- but you just aren't in their play field. They always seem just out of reach, right? It's like they are a whole different species. Just like your parents established- there are rich people, ... and then there are normal people like us. Two different classes- us and them.

Right?

As long as you see rich successful people as a different class than you, you will always remain separate from them, making just enough money to survive and not a penny more. Your

programming will not allow you to become one of "them"
because that would break your code (it's us versus them).
You don't want to become a greedy, selfish bad rich person now
do you? Some people are actually afraid deep down inside that
if they become rich, that they will give up a piece of their
soul ... that they "sold out" to the devil and not be respected
anymore by friends and peers. Sure, on the outside you will say
"Hogwash! No way", but deep, deep, deep down on the
emotional level, a hidden part of you is programmed to play it
safe and avoid becoming rich.

Have you ever had big money come REAL close, and then at
the last second it vanishes?

Have you actually made good money, only to have an
unexpected repair or emergency show up that took that exact
amount of money away again?

It's almost like some invisible thing is not allowing you to have
lots of money. But where is that coming from? Is the Universe/
God not wanting you to be wealthy? Is it better to remain
humble and righteous, rather than rich and evil?

Forget your greedy grabby mind and search your soul on a
deep, deep level. What kind of programming do you have?

I hate to break this to you- but there is no almighty force "out
there" keeping you from becoming rich, prosperous, happy and
successful. I used to think that. Oh, the brainwashing we get
from church, well-meaning parents, society and the media. The
bad guys in movies were always rich businessmen in three-
piece suits. Heroes were always poor down-and-out people

fighting the odds. We love rooting for the underdog and hating the upper crusty rich bastards, right? Right ? Uh huh. I was right there with you, buying all this crap. There is still a slight inkling tickling the back of my psyche right now. People we need a brain enema!

Heroes are always poor people? Come on. Puleeease.

So if you want to be respected in today's society, you better not be rich, right?

It's amazing. I love inspiring and educating people. I love making videos, DVDs and books (because I love them myself). These things cost money to make, and obviously I have to make some profit to pay my bills. Many of my followers are self-proclaimed "enlightened" people. But you would be amazed how there are always the few angry ones every time I come out with a book or DVD- they email me saying I'm only in it for the money, if I really wanted to help the poor, I should be giving this stuff away for free, or at least on a donation basis. They are angry miserable people who obviously aren't doing well and they are lashing out at others seemingly doing better than them. They want to pull everyone down to their level so they can feel good. Where does this come from? You guessed it- trace it back to early programming where the word "sell" is bad. "He's just selling something". (Yeah, so?)
Should all writers , musicians, artists, teachers, filmmakers etc work for free ??

Poverty consciousness is poison.

The thermometer of success is merely the jealousy of the malcontents. Salvador Dali

Money is not bad. It's just paper. Believe it or not, there is more than enough to go around for everybody. I'll bet that's starting to push your belief limits, but it's true. All you have to do is feel you deserve it, and then act on it. You have free choice. You can live up north where it's cold or do what I did- move south where there are palm trees, warm sand and blue open sky 360 days a year. It's staggering how many excuses and reasons people give for not being able to do that ("I have responsibilities, family, friends, job, children, school bla, bla, bla") You know what it really is stopping people from living their dream?

Fear of the unknown.

Look at your present money situation and compare it with what you grew up with. Did money come easy in your family or was it a constant source of stress? Did it flow steadily or come unpredictably here and there at random? Did things go good for a while, only to go back down to zero again each time? How does this compare with your situation now?

In order for you to change a pattern, you must first recognize it.

Once you expose something and see it for what it is, it no longer has power over you. Your chains fall away and you are finally free to fly.

If you think rich people screw the less fortunate then you will never be rich. This is a victim mentality. If you think "poor me", you will be poor.

You should have noticed in school every class or group has a loud, arrogant egotistical bully that picks on the less fortunate, but there were only a few of those in the group. Most of the class was normal, well-behaved people, many of them nerds that would end up being the next Bill Gates or Steve Jobs.

Rich people give more than you think... just not to you. And they have no obligation to give to you. They worked hard for that money and they can give it to whoever they want. Let's say you have $100. I'll bet you would rather give it to a loved one than to that bum on the street you ignored the other day, when he walked by your car and you looked the other way. You are not immune to favoritism. Rich people are no different than you. So don't resent them and <u>stop waiting for handouts,</u> because that's what keeps you poor. Stop being so comfortable in your pain.

Stop waiting for other people to save you

Your Dreams are Gifts

God, the Universe, whatever you want to call it, gave you dreams, talents, skills, abilities and unique traits for a reason. Almost everybody I've met has had a unique great idea for something. A new type of gadget, a new way to do something, a great idea for a book, the list is endless. But they were afraid to bring these new improvements to the world. Many of these people were the humblest poorest people, but their ideas were genius. Then I saw that the jobs they had and the things they did for money were NOT what they were. Their minds were so deep into other things they dreamed about, that they only did what was necessary to just get by. Their body was doing one thing but their heart and mind were somewhere else. They were undiscovered geniuses. I learned to not judge them just because they made minimum wage or did some sort of "demeaning" simple job.

Every living thing exists for a reason. It could be as simple as saying the right thing to the right person at the right time and changing their life forever. Maybe that was your purpose. Or it could be something as complex as building a healing center or bringing a new energy source to the planet or writing the next revolutionary book. We all have dreams, gifts and a purpose. But God/ the Universe also gave you free will, because a loving parent doesn't force a child to do anything. Just because you have the skills to become an artist, doesn't mean you have to become one. You are not obligated to do anything. You are free!

You also have the free will to be successful or not. Most people aren't aware of this. They just see themselves as followers of circumstance (i.e. victims). Now many of you will say "But I don't have any great skills, talents or abilities". Well you either haven't discovered them, or you repressed them a long time ago and forgot, or you saw them as worthless in the area of making money. It's amazing how many people sacrifice what they love doing in order to make money, so they become slaves to something that is not them.

Maybe you truly have no talent for anything, (highly unlikely). But I guarantee you that you have something no one else has. Something unique. Even if it's just a huge nose… it can make you famous.

But let me stop right here and say- it really doesn't matter.

Talent, skills and special abilities are great and may give you a perceived edge… but in reality, there are more super-talented people out there with no money wondering where their next paycheck will come from. I know because I was one of them.

Talent has very little to do with prosperity and success.

You can be the very best at something. You can have the best skills and knowledge. It doesn't matter. If your inner money programming is faulty, all the skills in the world aren't going to help you.

There are more untalented rich people out there than you can imagine. How many times have you wondered "How the heck did THAT person become rich?!?" You know you are better than them. Yet they are successful and you are not. Why? It just angers and frustrates you more.

Lesson Two
Stop the Jealousy and Frustration.

They will keep you poor. Never ever be resentful or angry at someone else for being more successful than you. I know this isn't easy, but do you want to become successful or not? The first thing you must do is clear your mind and completely throw away your opinions, anger, resentment, jealousy, suspicions, rumors, and anything else that falls into the category of negative emotions. They are poison. They will keep you down and poor. There are "poor" emotions and "rich" emotions. If you have both, they cancel each other out and you end up with nothing. If you are holding onto negativity, you will continue living in negativity. It's a very heavy emotion and nobody wants to be around a downer. If you want to fly with the angels, you must lighten your load, and the fastest way to do that is let go of negative emotions.

For example- you may look at some people with skepticism and say they are just trying to make a fast buck. Maybe they are, or maybe not. It doesn't matter. The important thing is you just had a negative thought, and that kind of thinking will KEEP YOU POOR ! If you keep looking for reasons to prove and validate your suspicions, you will always find them (if they are true or not) because that's all you will allow yourself to see. I will say that again.

You will always find what you are looking for. You will always prove yourself right. This is the world of quantum physics.

Do you realize the power of that statement? You can create any reality you want. Seek and ye shall find. Heck it's in the Bible. Seek and ye shall find. Good or bad. Seek and ye shall find.

If you think others are trying to rip you off... you are ultimately ripping yourself off with this stupid negative thinking. Misery loves company. Whatever lens you want to look through- that's what you will see, and nothing else. You cannot see green through red lenses. In other words, the green stuff (i.e. money) might be right in front of you, but you can't see it because you are looking through red (anger) lenses. If you have prosperity lenses on, you will see opportunity and prosperity in everything... and attract more and more of it. Why do you think the rich get richer and the poor get poorer? It's not all unfairness or mean people ripping off nice people. There are LOTS of nice wonderful kind-hearted rich people and lots of miserable nasty cruel poor people. It's the lenses people are looking through that allows them to see and attract more of what they see.

ABOUT ME

People think I got rich because I have skills and talents. Nothing could be further from the truth. Actually the opposite. I could paint before I could walk. By the time I was a teenager, I could draw and paint so realistically, people thought they were looking at photographs. I became so good at it, I could paint a photorealistic painting in one day. I had lots of talents, I could sculpt, paint, draw, design and build architectural wonders, complex electronic circuits, design and sew my own clothes, I won an automotive design contest, I pretty much could do anything in the fields of art, music, engineering, electronics, architecture, mechanics, literature, fashion, acting, photography, cinematography, computers, etc, etc, etc. BUT I WAS BROKE.

The more talent I discovered I had, the more broke I was. It was inversely proportional and it drove me crazy seeing so many untalented people out there rolling in wealth. So I tried harder. Hard work should certainly lead to success... right? Nope.

Lesson Three
Hard Work and skill does not mean success.

My parents worked really hard. I grew up on a horse farm and I learned to work hard. I could fix anything and do anything. I learned woodworking, electrical engineering, you name it. My parents worked morning till night. And they never became rich. I, of course, am a hard worker. For 30 years, the harder I worked, the less money I made (see a pattern?) I became the best at many things... but in reality, it just made me a glorified handyman. I was just seen as a service for hire. I worked in Hollywood as one of the fastest special effects artists and designers in the business. But I noticed something interesting. Almost all of the producers hiring me didn't have the talents I did. That's like an army commander not knowing how to fire a gun. How is this possible? I thought it was so unfair. The people doing all the hard work are the ones getting paid the least. I worked around the clock doing my very best and these successful producers came to work late, had two hour lunches and went home around 3 in the afternoon. Were they all simply born into rich families, or connected to the right people? They even told me they didn't have talents like me. As a matter of fact, many of them seemed down right Neanderthal. They seemed like lazy, spoiled egotistical lucky bastards. Now either the world is terribly unfair, or… or…. the rich people knew something we didn't. What is this perplexing magic they know… the less you work, the more money you make. Huh? If someone has talent, that's nice, but artists and musicians are a dime a dozen. But when someone says *"I'm putting a deal together"*… now <u>that</u> gets people's attention! Talented people usually end up working for people who put deals together. The people with the inspired vision- <u>those</u> are the big money people.

The Power of Magnetism

That's where I learned rich people use other people's research and ideas and put talented people together to make those ideas come to life. This is called a "Producer". They produce.
So you don't need skills or talent- you don't even need money. All you need is the wherewithal to put people, ideas and talent together, they do the work for you to create something the world wants and is willing to pay for.

Magnetic people attract. (money, other people, success) What is magnetism? It's an electric charge that activates a core. Let's take an electromagnet. It's a metal core with electric wire wrapped around it. When electricity (spark) is added to the wire, the metal core becomes magnetic. Coins attract to it. The same with magnetic people. If they have the "electric spark", people will attract to them, including talented people, smart people and workers willing to do anything.

Let me translate that for you. If you have the "spark", you will attract to you anything you need. You don't need talent. You will attract all the talent you need. You don't need money, skill, or details- that will all come to you if you have the right idea.

Lesson Four
Who you know does not guarantee success

If you hang around powerful people waiting for a handout, you are in it for the wrong reason and wasting everyone's time. They are not your ticket to success- You must blaze your own trail. I hear it all the time "My friend knows some big investors, I'll hook you up". How many people have wasted their lives waiting for others to come through? Too many to count.

Lesson Five
What you know does not guarantee success

Smart does not mean rich. People who think too much never get anywhere because their minds are always in the way. There are so many broke, lonely nerds out there, its become a cliché. All "Smart" means is someone memorized massive amounts of information- usually theories and opinions of other people, many of which get proven false after time. Being a human dictionary does not have anything to do with success. Thinking is a form of judgment. Poor people think. Rich people do.

"Omnipotence is not knowing how everything is done; it's just doing it."

- Alan Watts

Lesson Six
Being born into a rich family does not mean happiness.

Many persons have the wrong idea of what constitutes happiness. It is not attained through self-gratification but through fidelity to a worthy purpose.

Helen Keller

I spent twenty years in Hollywood hanging out with the rich and famous. A lot of the Beverly Hills brats are some of the emptiest most unfulfilled people I met. Just because they live in a big house, hang with the rich and famous and have lots of money does NOT mean they are happy. People do not appreciate what they haven't earned. They can have anything they want, but they don't know what. I've seen it over and over… all the money in the world and not knowing what to do with it. Ever wonder why so many stupid uncreative movies get made? Now you know why. It angered me seeing these spoiled rich kids getting millions of dollars to make movies and they simply make hollow copies of someone else's formula. The best movies usually come from people (writers, directors) who went through hell in life. They know hard times and what it is like to lose something beloved. The greatest movies usually involve human pain, and a hero is someone who has the strength to stand firm to what they feel, against all odds, and lose everything, but eventually triumph in the end. That's why Rocky was such a hit- the underdog beating the odds… that's

US!!! Look at the movie Titanic- love triumphs even over death. No spoiled rich brat can pull those kind of emotions because they don't know what it's like if they haven't been through hell and hard times. So learn this- those of us who had to go through pain have been set up for greatness. That pain happened for a reason! What doesn't kill us strengthens us and prepares us for winning any battle. We need fortitude and depth to endure the challenges of life. And those challenges never stop.

Being rich does not ensure stability. The world economy is proving that right now. If something is not built on a solid core foundation of truth and integrity, it is destined to collapse. Those smart stock brokers, bankers, MLM people and get-rich-quick business guys from the last twenty years are losing everything. Their world is falling apart because it was all built on nothing but greed and paper. Everyone wanted a quick fix, a fast buck, a big house, and the need to show off to impress their friends. Little did they realize their friends didn't care. If anything, it just irritated and frustrated them, or even worse, made them want to hang around hoping some of that wealth would rub off. None of that kind of living is genuine. Women would marry rich men thinking they had stability. People worked together not because they liked each other, but because someone had money or connections. This is all destined for failure.

We are entering a new world where that doesn't work anymore. The nation's economy is not important. YOUR personal economy is. A nation is just a collection of many personal economies, and the more successful individuals there are, the healthier a nation is.

People born into rich families may not appreciate what they have. Many of them may not be happy. They may even lose their wealth. But I can tell you one thing- odds are <u>they will make it back quickly</u> and always live a very, very comfortable life. Do you know why? Because to them, being wealthy is normal and to be expected, therefore they attract it easily without even trying much. This trait is what most people are lacking- the ability to feel comfortable with wealth and freedom. If "normal" people ever become wealthy, the challenge for them is to feel comfortable with it, and not have an underlying fear of possibly losing it again. Rich people don't fear loss or poverty. They know it will all come right back.

I don't know the key to success, but the key to failure is trying to please everybody.

Bill Cosby

WHY

The interesting thing is WHY people wanted big houses and fancy expensive stuff. Some people simply did it because that's what society said you needed to have a sense of accomplishment. But most people did it for one reason- they wanted to be ADMIRED, RESPECTED and LOOKED UP TO by others. When they were kids, they were picked on, beat up, made fun of, belittled and humiliated. Many didn't eat right so they became zit-faced ugly fat people. Some had dysfunctional parents who fought a lot and had money problems. Some were dreamers and didn't relate to the "normal" world. The reasons are many, but most people feel like outsiders, spending the first half of their lives in confusion and loneliness. It looks like everyone else is having more fun than us. The party is always "over there", not here where we are. Right? We have this life-long feeling we are missing out. Add to that all the years we were looked down upon by people "better" than us. We were made to feel like a lower class and all the fun was on the upper floors. Right ?

So when we DID get a bit of money, what's the first thing most people did? They got things to impress others to say "SEE- I'VE MADE IT... I'M JUST AS GOOD AS YOU NOW!" We strut our stuff and hope that finally we will be accepted and respected by others.

But others usually see right through that. It's not genuine. We are NOT our stuff.

Do you know what will really impress others? Seeing the REAL you. People want the truth. We are tired of wasting energy, running in circles. We want to be where we belong... as fast as possible. The time for bragging and hype is over. That's why reality shows are so big now. (the irony is most of them are staged and not really "reality"). Anyway, people want to see the real you, and they are willing to invest in reality because real things are solid guideposts to help others find their way by comparison. So what a relief that should be. You no longer need the flashy material things to win the admiration and respect of others. The real heroes now are the simple real people who aren't afraid to be themselves. They are not afraid to stand up for what they believe in, no matter what the cost.

Lesson Seven
We are not our stuff.

This is important. Prosperity and success does not mean lots of money, big houses, large bank accounts, private jets, freedom to travel, etc, etc, etc. Those are just side effects. Those just naturally come with the package. You CANNOT go after that stuff and think you are prosperous. Many people do everything they can (sometimes in regretful ways) to acquire that status, but when they get it, find a big emptiness. This is a HUGE important thing to learn right away if you truly want to become prosperous, successful and happy...

YOU CANNOT GO AFTER THE MONEY

IT NEEDS TO COME TO YOU.

Everything in the Universe is just energy. Everything. Your thoughts, your body, your lover and your money. Everything is just energy. It flows and is ever-changing. It is never the same and you cannot freeze it. Life is energy and movement. The only way you can be fully alive is to accept this flow and ride it …surf the wave of life. Anything you resist will break you because when you resist something, you become hard and brittle things break easily. Rubbery flexible things don't. The most successful people are flexible and willing to change with the flow at a moments notice. This does not mean they are flaky and get caught up in trendy fads. It means when they see Rome falling, they move to Greece. It means when they see something isn't working anymore, they are not afraid to let go of old ways of thinking and adapt to new ways of doing things. This is called progress. If this didn't happen, we would still be in the stone age. Not that stone age living is bad mind you, but if you want to enjoy a back rub in Australia before jetting to Bali to lie on a beach while writing your next novel on your laptop, you need to get with the times and flow with the new energies.

Once you learn that everything is just energy, and that going with the flow is key to success, you are well on your way to happiness. Now when I say "go with the flow" I am not saying to hop on the trendy bandwagon and do what everyone else is doing. That's small time. Most of those people are lost sheep. Someone yells "Hey the party is over here" so everyone runs over. Then someone yells "NO- the answer to your problems is over HERE" so all the sheep-people run over there.

No, the "flow" I am talking about is a much bigger one. It's the whisper of the Universe and the voice in your heart. The writing is always on the wall, but most people choose not to read it because there are so many loud people in the room screaming for attention or claiming they know the answer. We are constantly distracted. Many people spend their entire lives running from one trendy fad to another, and then they die tired, unhappy and empty. Don't let this be you. The best thing you can do is tune everyone out. Get rid of your T.V. Stop reading ads. Go somewhere quiet and start listening to that voice inside you. What is it saying? A great number of successful people turned right when everyone else turned left. They did something no-one else had done. They took chances. They listened to their inner voice.

That voice my friend is your guide to true success, prosperity and happiness.

The Voice

You have two voices. The one in your head, and the one in your heart.

The one in your head always makes the most sense. It seems "sensible" and is the one most people follow because it is logic-based. Logic is man-made. It is flawed. It is very seductive and will entice you with its great-sounding impressive reasons. I'm sure most of you have been sidetracked in life by a slick-talking salesman who made you invest in something that made a lot of sense at the time, but in your heart you never would have done so had you never met the guy.

I see this all the time with women and it really saddens my heart to see it. Women are loving, innocent right-brained creative beings that are flexible and open to new ideas. Men are left-brained, logic-based beings that think like computers. Everything to a man is numbers and statistics. They talk about how much horsepower a car has and how fast it can go from 0-60. Women couldn't care less about silly things like that. Men make great salesmen, because they rattle off all kinds of statistics and impressive sounding numbers. They are human encyclopedias of vast knowledge and facts and are very convincing. This impresses women and makes them easy targets for con artists- not just with money, but relationships. (I'm generalizing here, not everyone is like this obviously, but I see this a lot). Women are more organic, they live more on intuition and emotions.

Women are naturally wired to be truly successful, even more than men, but they just haven't had the chance to utilize their skills because until now, its been a male-dominated world. But that is all changing now. It has to, because the male-domination way of doing things is what's brought the world to the brink of disaster.

Time for Female Energy

I am not saying for men to completely step aside and let women take over, because logic has its place ..BUT the only way this world will heal and truly prosper is to finally let truth, honesty, gut feelings, emotions and the voice of the heart have a say in decision making. Women are gifted in this area, but their gifts have been repressed for centuries. The world cannot exist without balance. The game must be played fairly now. It's all energy. If the woman in a relationship is not allowed to blossom and have equal say, the prosperity factor in a relationship is doomed. Surely you've heard the phrase "behind every great man is a woman" (that helped make it happen). If someone in a relationship is unhappy or unfulfilled, that negative energy will ultimately poison any chance of true prosperity. Each person has something to offer. Each person has a piece of the puzzle. Walking requires two legs, not one. The time has come to not just walk anymore, but RUN. The world is speeding up. It's time to get serious. No more playing stupid mind games- the world needs truthful honest people working together as one. If you have the courage to be that, then you will be successful.

Prosperity is Energy

Have you ever noticed that when you sat around waiting for that important call to come through, it never did? But when you went on vacation or took a road trip or simply took off to be with family, that's when the phone calls started coming in? While you were gone? Why is that? OK, think about it. What were you doing when you were sitting around waiting? Nothing. And what were you doing when you took the road trip? You were MOVING. You were doing something. This is so important I should fill the whole page with this statement

Success is shy - it won't come out while you're watching. Tennessee Williams

YOU NEED TO MOVE !!!!!!!!

How do you get moving in life?

Get stuff done. - <u>ANYTHING</u>-

Just don't sit there and wait for that magic call. Start doing something that needs to get done. Fix that crack in the wall. Fix the washing machine. Clean up the yard. Go through everything you own and donate one third of it. I am not kidding.

The first lesson in energy is it needs to MOVE.

The second lesson in energy is you need to
<u>Make room for new energy.</u>

In this world it is not what we take up, but what we give up, that makes us rich.

Henry Ward Beecher

Let Go

One of the best things you can do is get rid of stuff. This is in my opinion one of the most important and powerful aspects of success. Remember- everything is energy and everything is connected.

Let's take a gum ball vending machine for example. Pull out the bottom one, and the next one takes its place. If you make a hole somewhere, something will fill it. Have you ever noticed there is no such thing as empty shelf space? The moment you set up a new shelf, table, box or any horizontal surface, almost immediately someone places something on it, like some temporary papers, keys, a drinking glass etc. The moment we make room, we fill that space with something, even if we think it's temporary storage space- the point is- space always gets filled. SO, like the saying says from the movie "Field of Dreams"- *"If you build it, he will come"*. This is so true. If you want to attract birds, put up some birdhouses with birdseed. If you want bees, plant flowers. If you want ANYTHING- start preparing for it right now. Make room for it. Put out the welcome sign.

You cannot attract new things into your life if your life is full of clutter. Is your house full of crap? Is your brain full of crap? Is your body full of crap? Is your job crap? Do you have crappy friends? What's your garage look like? How many clothes in your closet do you actually wear? How many of those yearbooks and photo albums do you ever look at? What about your old records, CDs and tapes? Come on folks- GET RID OF IT ALL!!!!! What do you really need? Do you feel like your life is stagnating? Do you want new energy in your life? MAKE ROOM! All that stuff you have is nothing but dead weight and stagnant energy. It is slowing you down. It has emotional baggage attached to it. If you want to fly, you need to lighten your load. This is not esoteric mumbo jumbo- it is hard truth.

In my book "Heal Yourself 101", one of the most important steps to curing anything- I mean any health condition you can imagine- is to clean out the body with fasting, water, juice-flushes, enemas and colonics. The body needs to be a clean, empty shiny tube from top to bottom- from mouth to anus. The moment anything stays stuck inside of us, it starts to rot and this is the beginning of disease. So the first step to true health- in body, mind, spirit , business, finances and any relationship- is to clean out. Our life needs a thorough flushing. If you want prosperity, you need a good life-enema. All the hard, crusty crap stuck in our lives needs to be washed out.

Simplify

"If you can't explain it to a six year old, you don't understand it yourself"
Albert Einstein

Your life is too complicated. Simplify it. Your energy is scattered in too many directions at once. No wonder you're overwhelmed and not making a lot of progress. Get rid of everything in your life you don't absolutely need. Shut off your brain for a moment and stop thinking logically, like "I might need this thing someday". No. If you don't need it right NOW, get rid of it. Sell it, donate it or throw it out. When you become prosperous, you can buy a newer, better one. The sooner you get into this mode, the sooner you will be freed up to be successful.

If you want a LOT of success, you need to make a LOT of room. Whatever you have now can be replaced with something newer and better. The only thing you need is your healthy body, integrity, love and freedom to be yourself. You can get all new clothes, the latest car, a new beautiful house, better friends and if need be, a more supportive relationship. Don't worry, genuine friends will always be there for you. But push this cleaning-out thing to the limit. Simplify your life like never before. This helps you focus.

Have a Purpose

The purpose of life is a life of purpose.
                                                    Robert Byrne

If you don't have a purpose, you are a depressed zombie. Living with intention is a driving force. If you don't have a goal or purpose, it means you are still distracted somehow.

So what is your purpose?

To be you.

It is truly that simple. It is the greatest honor you can give back to your creator. You were given unique traits that no one else has. What do you do with them? Listen to the signals- you are a radio antenna- you are constantly getting signals of what to do or not do, but most people can't hear them clearly, if at all, because there is so much static and noise in their lives. They can't concentrate with all the phone calls, talking, internet, bills, responsibilities, repairs and chattery (needy) family and friends. You can't think straight. Do whatever it takes to have some alone time so you can focus. When I wrote this book, I got in my car and took off to Palm Springs alone, found a cute little boutique hotel, and hid from the world so I could concentrate to write my book.

Sometimes you just have to walk away from your own life in order to clear your head and heart. It's hard to hear the inner voice when there are too many distractions.

Not eating and living right also interferes with your ability to receive signals. Your body is a giant antenna. It can receive sound, images, video, touch, smell, taste and psychic energy messages, but if your body is clogged up and not working right, you can't be a good antenna. It's amazing how clear you are when you have a newly cleansed body and mind.

No Fear

*"The greatest barrier to success
is the fear of failure."* Sven Goran Eriksson

I know what many of you are saying. "Oh that's easy for you to say Mr. Rich and Famous- you can just do what you want. Well we normal people have responsibilities and bills to pay" Bla, bla , bla. You know what that was? Excuses.

First of all, I was not always rich and famous. I was so down-and-out, there was a moment in my life where I actually lived in someone's closet for a few weeks. I am not kidding.

But you know what? When you have very little to lose- you have everything to gain.

*The pessimist sees difficulty in every opportunity.
The optimist sees the opportunity in every difficulty.*
Winston Churchill

Most people are in some kind of dysfunctional relationship (work, personal, finances, friends etc) but they still keep doing the same thing. I'm sure you've heard the saying "You can't expect different results by continuing doing the same thing" Yet people keep doing the same thing expecting something magical to happen to change it all.

Why are you fighting so hard to hang on to something that's not working?

One word. Fear. For most, it's better to hang on to something (even something crappy) than to have nothing at all. Right? Come on, ... right? We are afraid that we might not find something better out there. We hope our present situation will improve somehow. Or, it offers us some kind of perceived security. First of all, I hate to say this, but if you are waiting for someone else to change, you might be in for a long ride to nowhere because most people do not change. Humans are creatures of habit and once a pattern is established, it's very hard to break. Sure there might be a few superficial changes, but overall the person remains the same. You need to accept that right now.

Do not waste your time trying to change someone else. If they do change from your nagging, it will be temporary and they will resent you for forcing them to be something they are not. Change needs to come naturally on its own. All you can do is be a living example that will hopefully inspire others to change, but they must do it out of free will and only when they are ready- which is usually <u>not </u>fast enough for you.

I'm not saying to throw the baby out with the bathwater, but if you want to be successful, don't wait for someone else to do it for you, or even with you. You are on your own. Start without them. If they want to join you, they will, but don't count on it.

Even if you have fear, DO IT ANYWAY.

The Universe will give you what you ask for, but if you have fear or doubts, you void the shipment. For example- let's say you wish for a big investor... the Universe will send you one.

The moment it happens, you think "Wow, that was too easy. There must be a catch. What if this person is a scam? What if they're not for real? Can I trust them? What if they screw me? I don't want to be screwed. What if....? what if ...? what if...?" ... and the investment never happens. Well DUH- you energetically scared him away you pessimistic knucklehead! Who'd want to work with someone who doesn't trust them? What kind of relationship is that? Stop poisoning your opportunities with your fear and negativity.

Who wants to be around a negative doubting person? No one. Rich people are normal human beings just like you. They have the same emotions, including fear, BUT they don't let that stop them. They don't let the "what if's" drive them crazy. They don't let negativity paralyze them into inactivity. They act in spite of their hesitations and fear. Poor people on the other hand wait until the fear dies down (it never does!!). They put things off, they stall, they procrastinate and nothing ever changes so they give up and whine. You're either going to commit or you're not. And the more you wait, the less chance anything will happen, because each day that goes by adds more distractions that bury your idea until you won't even remember you had one.

Transcend and help pull people to your level. Don't let them pull you down to theirs

Don't Wait

You only wait for other people, not yourself. One of the biggest wasters of time is waiting for others. Stop waiting and start doing. The people who are right for you will come out of the woodwork when the time is right, you'll see. There is magic in doing. Just start walking. Others will join you. Just be aware it might not be the people you expected or hoped. You get what you need, not what you want. But don't let this discourage you. Maybe you thought you needed a Toyota and life said "No- this person needs a Mercedes!" So stop with the fear. You will always get what's right for you, and what you thought you wanted or needed may not have been the right thing, because that opinion was based on only what you knew.

If you wait, you'll never do it. So stop waiting.

The trick is to make sure you don't die waiting for prosperity to come. Lee Iacocca

Surrender to Success

The Universe can see a lot more than you can with your limited perspective of life. Trust and let go to the flow. Stop hanging on to something that's not working. Let the experts come in and upgrade your life, the Universe has been doing this a lot longer than you ...it knows what it's doing.

No Excuses

Excuses are a form of fear. They are a copout. If you have excuses, you won't be successful. Winners won't let ANYTHING stop them. If you say stuff like "I have to pay my mortgage, I have children, I have car payments, I have bla, bla, bla", then you are not thinking outside the box. As long as you are seeing yourself as a prisoner, you will never be free. If you want to escape your prison, you must be willing to take some chances. The prison guards will try to stop you, of course. There is always the fear of death (death of job, death of relationship-spouse might leave me etc). That is the great bluff. The Universe wants to see how serious you are. You need to prove your willingness to be a leader (of your own life) or else you will just be a follower (prisoner).

Again, everything is energy. Positive energy attracts positive energy and negative energy just brings everyone down. Why do you think they call non-prosperous times a "depression"? When people are depressed, it brings on... you guessed it- more depressing stuff and bad luck. Things break. Money is lost. It's a terrible downward spiral- one big magnet of negativity.

One of the worst things you can do is complain. I know it feels good to vent, but all you're doing is bringing other people down and creating more negative energy, which draws more negative stuff into your life to prove and validate how right you are. Whatever you focus energy on is what you attract. If all you do is complain, then you will attract more stuff into your life to complain about. Complaining makes you a magnet for bad luck.

If you want to improve your life, get away from complainers.
Negative energy is like a virus that can infect you and your life.
Stay away! Wish them well and move on with your life.

Many of the richest people became rich during hard times.
Why? Not because they are bad people and it's all a big
conspiracy, but because they see opportunity in everything.
They don't see negativity- they see opportunity. Sure, some
will take advantage of others, but there are both kinds. For
example, during the great depression, someone came up with
the bright idea to open a soup kitchen and make soup available
for pennies. It was an instant hit and that someone became rich.
Does this make them a bad person? Some will say "oh, he
should have given that soup away for free if he really cared".

The Self-Pity Poverty Conscious

I get that too. People sometimes say I should hand out my
DVDs or books for free if I really wanted to help the world.
Well this stuff costs money, and I have bills to pay also.

Any time you become a success, there will always be angry
negative unhappy people trying to pull you down to their level.
These people are stuck in a rut and will not be happy unless
everyone else is in the same rut with them. Misery loves
company. I'm sorry, but that's not where I want to be.
That is called poverty consciousness and most people have this
disease. They want the easy way out. They like to believe they
are victims of some big conspiracy they have no control over.
They like to swim in their own self pity and bring everyone
down. They love to blame everyone and everything for their

problems, and if you stick around long enough, they will probably start blaming you too. If you are financially better off than them, you are an easy target for resentment.

Let's look at this for a minute. What do they really want? If you gave them money, they would spend it and be right back where they started. They want to prove to you they are right, that they are victims and no matter what, the conspiracy-makers are out to get them. They want your pity. But what is pity? Think about it. They want ATTENTION- just like those people I mentioned earlier who bought all the status stuff so they could be respected and acknowledged by their peers. Pity is just another form of recognition. It is a drug and people can become addicted to pity like any other drug addict. It's a terrible trap to fall into. People end up doing stupid things to get attention. Bad luck happens to them and they don't make the connection why it's happening to them on a regular basis and not the people around them. If you try to tell them they are attracting it themselves they will probably try to rip your head off. It's a delicate situation, for sure. Maybe they should get a copy of this book.

Stop Feeling Sorry for Yourself

I do not pay any attention to people who want attention. It actually angers me when someone has a "poor me" attitude and wants pity. I refuse to give them the time of day. That's called enabling. My heart goes out to people who don't feel sorry for themselves and have a smile <u>DESPITE their situation</u>. It's a hard lesson, and the sooner people realize the only one who's going to pull them out is THEMSELVES, the sooner they are on their way to freedom and happiness.

Comfort

This way of thinking creates mental patterns. Remember - humans are creatures of habit and habits are hard to break. One of the patterns we create is comfort level. Many people are "trained" to be comfortable with little or no money. They don't feel comfortable with a lot of money. If you gave it to them, they wouldn't know what to do with it or how to handle it. You see this all the time- poor person wins lottery, blows all the money and ends up broke again.

On the other hand- rich people are the opposite. They are "programmed" to be comfortable with the rich life. No matter what happens to them, they always end up at the same place. Donald Trump went broke half a dozen times but always bounced back. People will always end up where they feel comfortable. Sure most people will say they want to be rich and have the good life, but somewhere deep inside, there is a little nagging feeling that

1- it's probably not going to happen
2- if it did, it probably won't last
3- the government would probably take most of the money
4- people would be jealous and not like them anymore
5- life would become too complicated
6- etc, etc, etc

Do you see a common theme in those thoughts?

They are all negative. Deep down inside, the person has already sent the message out to themselves and the universe that they are not too excited about being rich. They've already shot themselves down before anything can happen. This is the exact opposite of how a rich person thinks. If you want to become prosperous, you MUST change this programming.

Where does this programming come from?

Everywhere. Your cynical parents- *"rich people are bad. They are vultures, leeches, scum. They are the cause of the world's problems"* bla, bla, bla. Look at movies and television from the last 100 years- the bad guys are usually rich. Right? Overall, people hate the rich. Why would we ever want to become something that most people hate? Think about that. Back to square one- we want to be accepted, loved and adored, right? We want all the poor peasants to look up to us as a hero, and that can't happen if we are in a castle high above them. This underlying feeling will undermine any chance of becoming affluent and prosperous... because we think people will hate us and there goes all that respect we worked so hard to achieve all our lives.

Let's go back to the colored glasses. When we are wearing "poor man's glasses" we only see poor people, so they become our world. They are the ones we want respect from. We do whatever we have to in order to win the poor man's respect. We think there are only a few rich people on top of the hill and they are all cold heartless scum.

But if we put on "rich man's glasses" we start to see a whole new world... wow- where did all these rich people come from? I thought there were only a few! Yes that's right folks- there are more millionaires out there than you could ever imagine, even in this economy, and they are multiplying every day. And guess what? Many of them are really nice people! They seem different than the others. They seem classier, they don't use gutter language as much, they seem more relaxed, they are friendly, they don't say all kinds of negative stuff like those poor people do. Hmmmm. Wow, what an eye opener. Rich people are not all bad! As a matter of fact, MOST of them are really, really nice.

This is where you realize money is just an amplifier. If you are a bad person, it makes you a more powerful bad person, but if you are a good person, you have much more power to do good for the world ...plus you can now do whatever you want- like take vacations in Fiji.

Think Rich

So the first thing we need to do in order to join the rich and prosperous is start thinking like them.

If your brain just flashed the word "greedy" or "selfish" or "cold" etc, then you just caught yourself in the act of remaining poor. You just exposed your inner programming. This is faulty programming put in there many years ago by your parents and brainwashed into your brain by society. Well look at society-take a good look- it's pretty messed up. It's falling apart. People are unhappy and dying by the millions... and you are listening to this society? That's like following the advice of a drug addict or schizophrenic nutcase.

Most of you have no clue what the rich are really like. The only thing you know is what you've been told or seen on TV. I have known rich people my whole life and I can tell you first hand they are no different than you and me- except for a few minor things. And these things make all the difference in the world between being rich or poor.

The Rich Perspective

The first thing I noticed is how calm and polite the rich are.

Now you will jump in and say "Oh yeah, that's easy when you're rich- they don't have any worries".

First of all- if you had a thought like that- you just caught yourself in yet another "stay poor" pattern. That's negative energy, and nothing will keep you poor faster than negative thoughts, sarcasm and anger.

Like I said earlier- the rich are programmed a certain way. The reason they are calm and polite is because they THINK THAT WAY. Let me rephrase that. They think positive. Even when they are broke. I know, because I am like that. No matter what happens, there is always an underlying optimism. Even when I was living in that closet, I still had optimism, hope and peace, because I knew this was temporary.

The rich are comfortable not because of their money, but because they are comfortable WITH THEMSELVES. They are not afraid to be themselves, say what they feel, and stick to their feelings and beliefs. Money is just a side-effect of being content with yourself. You don't go after the money- you go after integrity. It's really not that hard, once you've done it for a while. It's like a muscle. The more you use it, the easier it gets and the less fear you have to be yourself.

There is only one success - to be able to spend your life in your own way.

Christopher Morley

You might say many rich people don't have integrity, they are heartless and rip people off. There are always bad seeds, even among the poor. But life is a movie and some of the bad guys play their role well. They actually have integrity at being a bad guy and sticking to it. Once you see them as actors playing their role well, you smile and actually appreciate their skill because once you see them for what they are, they are no longer a threat to you. Anyway, my point is- the rich are comfortable with themselves. They do what they love.

It's better to be hated for what you love, than to be loved for what you are not

Andre Gide

Most poor people on the other hand are doing things they hate, thinking that someday it will all change (it usually never does).

This can all change though. All it takes is a change of perspective. You need to be able to let go of everything you are used to. Theoretically, it shouldn't be that hard to change since you are unhappy with what you have- you would think. But the amazing thing is most people hang on for dear life to their dysfunctional lives because it's all they know. They would rather have something dysfunctional than nothing at all. That "nothing at all" part is impossible. You will always have something.

When I was naked in the desert, with literally NOTHING, no house, no money, no phone, no agenda, no plan, no bills, no appointments, no-one waiting for me, no-one to answer to or worry about... I was never more alive than that moment. It was exhilarating. If the rabbits, turtles, birds and lizards around me could exist happily, then so could I. They had care-free lives, basked in the sun, had sex three times a day, slept, wandered, played and relaxed. No mortgage bills, no stress. I learned to eat the wild plants and realized everything we need is supplied to us by nature. We will never starve.

We are taken care of, even when we have nothing.

This is a major realization. When you realize you will never starve, your confidence level radically changes. This changes the playing field. Now you can start taking risks like never before. Sure you may lose your house, car, job and friends... but so what?! There are millions more out there, many of them newer, better models than what you had before. It becomes kind of an exciting game. When life takes something away from you it usually gets replaced with something better. Which flavor will it be today? We are here to experience life and all its flavors. Don't get hung up on one thing, especially if it has issues.

Your Mirror

Now don't get me wrong. When it comes to the relationship with my mate, I am steadfastly committed with intense romantic passion. We will always have issues and differences because no two people are the same, so I expect that. I see them as a sounding board, sparring partner, best friend, conscience, mirror and nemesis. It's so important to have someone not afraid to say what they see and feel. Most people don't have the guts to tell you there's a booger hanging out of your nose. Don't look for a mate with all perfect qualities, they don't exist. Perfectionists are unhappy people. Your mate is a special gift to help you see yourself in ways you probably never would on your own. They come into your life at the right time, and when they have done their job, they move on. This isn't a failure, it's a completion. Each year in school we have a different teacher.

Like rich people, you need to be comfortable with what is. You need to be comfortable knowing that at any time you may lose everything, and that's ok. Because that frees you up and makes room for the next, newer, upgraded model, whatever it is... house, car, job, hobby, friends, relationship etc. Don't be in a hurry. Whatever you have in your life, appreciate it fully, every moment. Taste every morsel of life like it was your last, because it might be. That way you will have no regrets.

Life is not about money, it's about appreciation. Focus on what you have, not what you don't have.

The more comfortable you are with yourself, and the more you appreciate all the wonderful little magic moments in life- the little hummingbird outside, the beautiful ray of warm sunlight kissing your skin, the soft breeze playing with your clothes, the feeling of someone's hair, the sound of their breath, the look in their eye... only then can you ever be ready for prosperity. Life will not hand you bigger gifts if you can't even appreciate the small ones. Would you give a million dollars to someone who doesn't appreciate it? Of course not. So why would life give it to you? And guess who runs your life? That's right. You.

You see, there is the outer you that says you deserve everything. Then there is the quiet inner, more realistic you that knows you are not ready yet, and will only attract success when you are ready.

Making yourself ready isn't that hard if you stop resisting the unknown. Replace fear with excitement. Override logical thoughts with gut feeling, because things are not always what they seem, no matter how logical it sounds. Life is a big movie and a lot of what you see is merely a facade. What people say isn't always the truth. The real truth is in your gut and heart.

Rich people think differently. They are winners and think like winners. They are bold. They attack life even if they feel fear and go after the best because they know and feel they deserve the best. They make money to be free and do what they want.

Poor people on the other hand make money to "pay bills" or "survive" or as "security". They are defensive. When they go out, they use coupons or buy only stuff that's "on sale" and try to find the cheapest thing that can get the job done. They like to use the term "counting pennies." Do you see the difference?

Poor people want.
Rich people do.

You see things and you say, 'why?'
but I dream things that never were;
and I say 'why not?'"
Thomas Edison

The only difference is the mindset. You don't need to know
HOW something is going to happen, you just need to feel that it
WILL. You don't need to know the details, the Universe will
take care of that. You just need to know what you want and you
need to confidently CLAIM IT. It doesn't matter if you are flat
broke- you can wake up one day and say "I'm getting a Ferrari.
I don't know how, but I'm getting one." I did. It works. One
of the biggest reasons people don't get anywhere is because
they don't know what they want.

I will say this again. You don't need to know the details. All
you need is to know what you want. It needs to be for the right
reasons and have POSITIVE energy attached to it. If there is
any doubt, guilt, worry, fear or second thoughts attached, it
won't happen. You need to be pure.

Remember when I said I lived in my friend's closet for a while?
It was after I went out into the desert naked and gave up
everything I owned. I had my forty days and came back a
changed person. I had to start somewhere, so it was a friends

closet. Within one month, I was driving a Ferrari (with no help from anyone).

If I can do this, so can you.

All it takes is the right frame of mind. Only positive energy, no negative thoughts whatsoever. It's hard to get this way when you have lots of crap in your life. That's why it was easy for me when I had nothing. I was clean. I was pure. Once you've accepted death, you are given life.

Do you feel rich or poor?

The rich feel rich even when they don't have a penny to their name, because they know they will get it back.

The poor feel poor, even when they have money in the bank, because they know it will probably get spent or taken away again.

One thinks positive and one thinks negative. Which are you?

Obstacles are those frightful things you see when you take your eyes off your goal.

– Henry Ford

Rich people see possibility in everything. Poor people see obstructions, drawbacks, limitations and risks. Rich people envision greatness, poor people envision what could go wrong. One is confident optimist, the other is defensive pessimist. Rich people take action. Poor people procrastinate out of fear.

This reprogramming is incredibly difficult for most, sometimes impossible because of deeply ingrained programming, fears and thought patterns.

But it can also be quick and easy. As a matter of fact, the change can happen in a millisecond- in a magical AHA moment- a life-changing flash of inspiration.

The choice is up to you. How willing are you to let go?

I mean REALLY let go.

You must immediately stop blaming others for your situation.

You must immediately take FULL responsibility for your life.

You must let go. Fear is replaced with excitement.

Anger, frustration, resentment, sarcasm and skepticism is replaced with hope, laughter, love, desire to help, grow, learn and do the right thing, whatever the cost. If you lose everything, that's ok. You need to be fully ok with that. You need to be a leader, not a follower.

Successful people jump out of airplanes without a doubt that their parachutes will open. Most others will say no thank you and not even get on the airplane. If you want to soar, you need to get on that airplane, otherwise you will spend your whole life on the ground bitterly looking up as others fly over your head yelling "yeehaaaaa".

Did you just have a moment of bitter jealous resentment for the "others" when I said that? Or did you get excited? That should tell you where you are at. In order to become that new person you want to be, you must first know where you are at.

Angry people attract more things to be angry about. Happy people attract more things to be thankful for. Notice I didn't say anything materialistic or money-related. Remember, money and rich stuff are only side-effects that come to you when you have the right frame of mind. Step one is to STOP all negative thinking and find peace in your life.

Just like in my health book Heal Yourself 101, you start by stopping all the things that are bad for you. You can't put out a fire if you are still trickling gasoline on it. So how do you stop negative thinking? You get rid of everything that's making you miserable and burdening your life. If it's heavy mortgage payments, get rid of your house. Many people are losing their homes now because of the bad economy. Years from now, many will see that as one of the best things that could have happened to them, because it took a big burden off their shoulders.

Do you hate your job? Leave it. Find something you love. "Easier said than done" you say? Well if you said that, then it's true for you because that's negative energy and I just caught you again keeping yourself poor. If you've been in the same job for years, barely making ends meet- what on earth makes you think that if you keep doing the same thing that you will somehow magically become rich?

Life is testing you. It's about taking chances.

What's that you said? You have children?

So?

Why is that stopping you? You need money to feed them and pay for medical bills? Well if they didn't eat bread, pasta, cereal, candy, milk, sugar, soft drinks and all that other unnatural crap, they wouldn't have any medical bills because they'd be healthy from day one. Anyone who's watched my FREE FOOD AND MEDICINE dvd set knows the healthiest food and medicine on the planet is free- it's the wild plants growing in your neighborhood. Crazy and unrealistic you say?

Watch my FREE LIVING 101 dvd set- about a man who lives in a normal suburban home in Toronto Canada (where it snows in the winter), and doesn't need a grocery store because he lives off wild plants living all within one mile of where he lives, makes enough money recycling to pay his mortgage, utilities, and even has enough left over to buy two more properties! All his health problems went away after living off wild plants.

There is NO EXCUSE.

If you want to get better, you need to STOP doing what's bad for you. Fully commit. If you want to be truly free, then truly free yourself of EVERYTHING that is holding you back, slowing you down, depressing your mood, or distracting your attention from being who you are on this Earth to be.

Twenty years ago, I literally got rid of everything I owned... everything, went out to the desert, took my clothes off and started over. I told people I didn't even know if I was coming back. I literally gave up and cleared out until I had no more expectations, no more anything. I laid naked on a rock and said "God- here I am". I cleared my mind and closed my eyes.

The greatest moment in someone's life is the moment before they die, because that's the moment you give up, you totally let go. No more fear- you totally accept the truth. It is the most freeing moment of your life.

The trick is to not wait, and feel that feeling <u>every moment of your entire life</u>! That my friends, is living. To never be afraid again. To follow your heart and do and say whatever feels right. When you start clean like this, every moment is a gift. You appreciate every breath, every sight, every sound, every touch.

This is where you must end up to truly start over.

In order to replace negative thinking, you need to start appreciating everything in your life, even the "bad" things. Start every day only looking for things to be thankful for. Don't put any energy into things that normally would have bothered you. When you think about something, you are "feeding" it. Remember, it's all energy. If you are thinking or dwelling on something that bothers you, or something you fear might happen, you are "feeding" that and strengthening it, thereby bringing it into existence and actually making it happen.

If you are going to spend any energy, you might as well use it thinking positive stuff, because thoughts make things happen.

What would you attempt to do if you knew you would not fail? – Robert Schuller

Thoughts make things happen.

Watch your thoughts; they become words.
Watch your words; they become actions. Watch
your actions; they become habits. Watch your
habits; they become character. Watch your
character; it becomes your destiny.

- Frank Outlaw

Never say "what else can go wrong", because you'll find out.

Thoughts are like friends at school. If you stop hanging out with the bad kids, they will slowly fade out of your life. The more you hang out with the good kids, the more you start getting strength from them. The same goes with your thoughts, The less time you spend thinking about the bad things that might happen, the less power they have in your life until one day they are totally gone and forgotten.

Spend time thinking about the wonderful things. Feed them. Water them. Nourish them. Fertilize them. They are your future.

Remember- money is not a goal, it is a side effect from doing what makes you happy.

Success is not the key to happiness. Happiness is the key to success. If you love what you are doing, you will be successful.

Your purpose, your mission, your JOB, your duty... is to be yourself. Integrity has nothing to fear.

Luck is Not Random

Do not for one second think all those rich people out there are "lucky". Luck is not random. It is created.

People who believe in luck feel they are not in control. They spend their whole life buying lottery tickets hoping to get "picked". Rich people don't wait, they simply go after what they want, even if they have no money. The journey of a thousand miles starts by putting a foot forward and start walking. You create your own future.

The Moment That Changed Everything

I was in Bombay, India preparing to shoot a movie I wrote, but for some mysterious reason, the money never came through. Even the producers mysteriously disappeared without a trace. I now know why. Because this was a strange situation. Bombay is very poor and I had doubts that anything would come of this... and because I had those doubts, my energy of my thoughts created the reality to prove my thoughts right. In other words, my (negative) thoughts killed my project. The mind is more powerful than you can imagine. I've caught myself doing this numerous times throughout my life, until I learned better.

To make a long story short, I was stranded in Bombay, India. I had invested everything I had to go there and make this movie. My assistants were getting worried. I had to pay for them and the hotel. Every day that went by cost me almost a thousand dollars. We decided to break up and find our way back to America, but it wasn't easy to get flights. With almost no money left, all we could get was a flight to Singapore. After negotiating with the airlines we made it to Hong Kong, then two days later, Vancouver Canada, and after being stopped by customs because we hadn't slept in days and looked terrible, we finally scratched together a flight to Los Angeles with the last few pennies we had. I arrived back at my apartment broke, tired and speechless. Why was my life just ripped apart? Nobody in town had any work for me and I had no way to pay my rent. I was confused, bummed out and lost.

I'm sure many of you are feeling similar emotions right now.

Sure I was speechless and maybe I had a moment or two of fear and confusion. But I let it pass right through me. I didn't hold on to those emotions or feed them. I just cleared my head, my body and my energy and just sat there refusing to dwell in anything that resembled helplessness.

As a matter of fact, I completely shut off my chattery mind of any immediate responsibilities, like how to pay bills etc.

I needed to feel good. I couldn't afford to get a massage or anything, so I allowed my mind to slip into fantasyland.

I imagined a gleaming white castle high up above the clouds where art and beauty were cherished. This was a place where artists and musicians could thrive, never having to worry about money. Everyone was beautiful and healthy. This is where I wanted to be. This was my escape.

Being the imaginative person I am, and seeing life as a movie, I imagined flying ships coming to attack this castle (this was the outside "real" world trying to attack my freedom and dreams).

But the castle was ready. This castle was my imagination, so all kinds of imaginary weapons unfolded from the castle- like they were designed by Leonardo Davinci- giant gears, pulleys and ropes maneuvered things in towers and turrets. Gargoyle lion heads opened their mouths revealing cannons inside. I let my imagination run wild. It was fun.

Then I realized what was happening. I was channeling a movie! I could see every shot. I could hear the music. The story poured into my head. I grabbed pen and paper and started jotting everything down as fast as I could, but it started coming too fast, so I ran and bought a cheap laptop at Radio Shack and immediately started typing the story. It poured through me as fast as I could type. I was amazed at what was coming through me. This was too detailed and extensively thought out to be something I was just making up. This was a divine download being entrusted to me by the Universe. It must have been because my resistance was down and I had given up.

When you get out of the way of yourself, the greatest stuff starts coming through, and the Universe will give you as much as you can handle!

The story was amazing and <u>I knew this was going to get made</u>.

* * * * This is the moment everything changed * * * *

Most people would look at this and think "How the heck am I going to make a freaking motion picture when I can't even pay my bills and there are no jobs anywhere?"

That's how most normal people would think, but not crazy Markus. Thank God I had an understanding girlfriend who stood by me no matter what, no matter how crazy the idea. She wasn't afraid to live on the edge. It was exciting. We kind of knew deep down inside we would always be taken care of. Bills, debt, rent and credit issues come and go. Even rich people have them. One minute they're up, then next they're down. But they never let it keep them down. The same with me.

Something happened in me that day. It was like that moment in "Grinch Stole Christmas" where his heart magically grows and he becomes a new person.

I knew this movie was going to get made. I could see it, hear it, feel it. It wasn't "Gee this would be great if it got made someday", no it was "I am going to make this movie! I don't know how, but I am making this movie, whatever it takes. I'm tired of waiting for others. I'm doing this myself. I'm going to make this happen and I'm doing it right now!" My logical mind was shut off, so I didn't have anything telling me I was crazy and making no sense. I was committed. It was resonating in my cells.

I wasn't concerned HOW I was going to pull it off, all I knew was I just signed a contract with myself and I was on my way to making a movie.

It was at that very moment that my whole life changed.

I could feel it. When you make the right decision, every cell in your body vibrates. You feel fully alive. You feel invincible because you are. You have the entire Universe behind you. You can feel it patting you on the back saying "Good work Markus, you passed the test! We just wanted to make sure you were serious and committed before we invested in you.

You see, the magic happens the moment you commit fearlessly with no way out. No turning back. All or nothing.

People don't invest in you, the Universe does.

And like any sensible shrewd investor, it will not give you anything you aren't serious about. It also won't give you anything you can't handle. Sure you may WANT a million dollars- but can you handle it? Really? You can't lie or cheat the Universe- it knows you better than you know yourself.

Would you give the keys to your car to a six year old? Of course not. Would you give a nine year old a million dollars? No. Why? Because they aren't ready to handle it yet. The Universe treats you the same way. You can jump up and down and throw all the temper tantrums you want, but it's not going to give you a million dollars if you aren't ready.

Remember- if you build it, he will come. But only when you are ready.

We usually wait for others to solve our problems for us.

We wait for others to give us money.

The Investor

As a shrewd, smart investor-

-would you simply give money to someone who's just sitting there waiting for a handout?

-would you invest in someone who's trying really hard to make something happen, but not having a lot of luck?

- or would you invest in someone who is totally gung-ho and making it happen on their own with or without you?

Which one would you have the best shot at for getting a return on your money? Number three of course. The universe is not stupid. It doesn't invest in losers, lazy bums or people with a flawed plan that's not working well.

It's also not going to give money to someone who says "Money is not important." Would you? Why give something to someone who doesn't appreciate it?

I was tired of waiting for others to come through with money for my ideas, so I was going to simply get it myself. It's amazing how things come to you when you are fired up. I didn't know a lot of people, but I knew that the landlord that owned my apartment complex owned half of the city block I was on. I knew a couple of doctors and a lawyer or two. I knew they had lots of money and could easily invest 50 or 100 thousand if they had to. They also have rich friends who are the same, so if I got a dozen of them to each invest up to 100 thousand, I had a million dollars. It was so easy. I could feel it!

I knew this was attainable. I was so convinced, I started drawing up the plans, sketches of the sets, costumes, everything.

Success is the progressive realization of predetermined, worthwhile, personal goals. Paul J. Meyer

One of my friends called me up and said "hey, I can get this to a film company, let's see if they'll fund it". I told him I had heard that a thousand times before and was tired of it. No more Hollywood games. I'm doing this on my own. But he persisted and said "they are literally just one block away from you- come on, this will just take ten minutes! It's only one block away!"

I was so fired up doing it on my own, I decided to have the meeting, but only because I was looking forward to finally telling Hollywood "I don't need you!", which is exactly what I did. I burst into that office with a determination I never had before. I had no patience anymore. I looked that producer straight in the eyes and told him I was tired of all the Hollywood BS and I was getting my landlord, doctor and lawyer friends to each pitch in a bit of money and I was going to do this on my own. The producer saw I was serious and knew I was going to make this movie with or without him. It was obvious. He smiled. He was the eyes and ears of the universe.

Normally in the past, I would go into a meeting just like everyone else on my knees all humble and wishful, hoping that I would be the lucky one they would invest in. That kind of submissiveness is a turnoff to people with power. They only respect other people with power. That's why they keep using established people and not newcomers.

But this time, I was in the power position and he knew it. He said "Just let me read the script tonight, I'll call you in the morning". He did. He liked it. He told me to forget going to all those small investors, he can fund the whole movie outright, one million dollars.

Within one week the contract was signed.

Within three weeks we had our first check.

Within two months, the budget got raised to 2.5 million.

I was the director of my own Hollywood motion picture! I had four hundred employees working for me, bringing my dream to life- set builders, costume designers, stunt people, great actors, a philharmonic orchestra with 100 man choir doing the soundtrack- knights on horseback in Death Valley, epic battle scenes, pyrotechnics, special effects- you name it.

From zero to 2.5 million- all because something inside me clicked.

I believed in myself.

This is the magic moment. The key to success. Committing all or nothing to yourself with life or death determination. This is what every investor wants to see- someone willing to do whatever it takes, no matter what. Someone so driven to succeed, they will do so with or without you. The moment you commit everything- all or nothing- to yourself- you will have the power of the entire universe backing you up and working through you.

The "you" that you are believing in is actually the Universe, disguised as "you". It wants to make sure you are willing to go all the way. No investor will invest in a spineless uncommitted wimp. Investors want to see strength and total commitment in the people they invest in. The Universe is your investor. It has more power, more money, more resources than you could ever dream of and ever need. But it will only give you what it thinks you can handle. And you have to PROVE you are worthy of whatever you are asking for. You can pound your chest and scream to the world you have what it takes, but if you secretly have ANY doubt whatsoever inside yourself, the universe can see it, just like any animal can smell your fear. You can't hide the truth. You can trick others, but not yourself and not the universe. Whatever you believe or fear becomes your reality. Doubt and fear is the greatest hindrance of any success. This is what the bible talks about- are you willing to sacrifice yourself to God (i.e. the truth, the Universe), because if you are, you will have unlimited power. This means letting go of ego and selfish motivation. True power comes from selfless commitment. And when you feel your whole body vibrating with excitement, that means you have aligned with the power of the Universe. You hit the magic sweet-spot of success.

When an army sees its Captain bravely charge the enemy by himself, what happens? Suddenly an overwhelming energy overtakes the entire army. They don't think anymore- they just act and charge also, following the courageous Captain. The Universe is your army and it's waiting to follow you into battle. But you must lead the charge. No more fear. This is it.

You become a millionaire the moment you decide to become one. Once you claim it, the money starts following.

Get out of the way
and let the experts do the work.

The only thing in the way of your success is you. The experts are God aka the Universe. They see more and know more than you ever will. They created you and work through you. Trust them, after all, they made you !

Plus it's a lot less work when you let them do all the work. All you have to do is go along for the ride. All the Universe wants is for you to be YOU! How hard is that? You are the lead hero actor in your own movie. Be a great you. That's all.

Its amazing how scared most people are to be themselves. They don't have the courage to tell their closest loved ones how they really feel. They spend most of their lives living a lie. And they are ultimately kidding no-one but themselves. Most people can see right through your facade. So stop wasting your energy putting up a fake you, trying to win everyone's approval. You're only wasting valuable days, weeks and years.

What people really want is the real you. And they are willing to pay for it. It is the Universe rewarding you. You don't get anywhere with hope. You get there with self-determination.

Let me rephrase the opening sentence- the only thing in the way ...is the way.

Life is either a daring adventure or nothing.

Helen Keller

Body Health and Money Health

<u>is the Same Formula</u>

As I was writing my book Heal Yourself 101, I realized an amazing correlation.

Only a tiny, tiny fraction of people in the modern world are truly totally healthy. Maybe 5%, probably closer to 1%.

Most people that claim to be healthy, really aren't. People seem to equate being vegetarian as being healthy. No, all it means is they don't eat animals, that's all. Vegetarians are some of the unhealthiest people I see. They eat bread, pasta, cereal, cookies, crackers, protein bars, and all kinds of cooked, processed crap that does nothing but rot their malnourished bodies.

Even many raw-foodists have weaknesses. They eat mainly sweet stuff and not enough greens. They are obsessed with what goes in their mouth and how it tastes, but pay little attention to seriously cleaning out their bodies (colonics, enemas etc). If you really want to get healthy, you need to clean out and let go of your addictions and the accumulated crap you are carrying around. There is no way around this.

Over 95 percent of people in the modern world are unhealthy, possibly even as much as 99 percent. Everyone has weaknesses and cheats somehow somewhere when no one is looking.

The irony is ...most people KNOW what's good for them. This is the 21st century- communication is instant. Anything you want to know is available at your fingertips on the internet. The old line "gee I didn't know" no longer holds water. At some point in our lives we have been told the truth- we just chose not to pay attention and conveniently tuned it out. Most people choose comfort and convenience over longevity, because instant gratification is so easy and seductive nowadays.

(Stick with me here, this has everything to do with wealth)

Most unhealthy people KNOW that apples, salad and vegetable juice are healthier than pizza, cereal and bread. So why don't they do it? Because they are stuck in addictive patterns of instant gratification and comfort. It's easier to plop into a cozy armchair than to jog around the neighborhood. It's more fun to eat a quick bowl of crunchy cereal than pull out the juicer and run celery and carrots through it. We want to push a button and feel good instantly. This is the modern world.

The same goes for wealth and prosperity.

I can take the same wording I used above in health and simply replace it with wealth-

Only a tiny, tiny fraction of people in the modern world are truly totally wealthy. Maybe 5%

Most people that claim to be wealthy, really aren't.

Over 95% of the world is not rich.

(see how similar these two categories are?- amazing huh?)

So what is the common denominator here?

People.

I will say this again. The 5% are NOT conspiring to keep the 95% poor. I am so tired of hearing that. Sure some of them might be trying, and yes wars are fought using people as pawns so the ones in charge can stay in power and all that. Yes that is happening, but not everywhere. The world is much bigger and more diverse than that. There will always be bad guys, but there are just as many poor bad guys. Most gangs, drug dealers, pimps, murderers are not wealthy. There are a few on top living the high life, but most are not. This formula is pretty unanimous across the board, so stop with the rich being different than the poor. Money doesn't corrupt- it just intensifies what you are. Take any inner-city drug dealer and give him millions of dollars and he simply becomes a very rich powerful drug dealer with yachts and airplanes. Yes there are lots of corrupt people in government, but not all of them are.

I know lots of rich people. Trust me. Those people in Beverly Hills do NOT sit around spending their time figuring out how they can screw the less fortunate. They are too busy getting spa treatments, facelifts and botox injections. They don't want to screw the poor people- they want to be adored by them. People want respect and adoration. That's really all anybody wants, even the rich drug dealer.

OK, let's get back on track. 95% of the world we see is not rich. Let's reword that - "not healthy in the wealth department"

Wealth is a form of health.

Most people are not "healthy" in the wealth category.

...for the very same reason 95% aren't healthy physically.

Both sides KNOW what is better for them.

But they don't do it.

... why?

Come on, you should know this by now-

...because they are stuck in addictive patterns of instant gratification and comfort. It's easier to plop into a cozy armchair than to jog around the neighborhood. It's easier to continue doing a job we hate than take a chance of losing everything and starting over. Maybe we hate our job, but at least it pays for the things that give us instant gratification... the cozy armchair, pizza, cereal, electricity to watch sports on TV, gasoline for the monster truck outside with the big manly tires so we can impress our neighbors. Ooh, yeah, that's living.

This is the modern world.

The rich 5% are not afraid to stick their necks out and take risks. They are not attached to their "things" because the world is their playground. The poor on the other hand desperately hang on to the few pitiful things they have, because they are afraid they might not have anything if all gets taken away. This fear of poverty KEEPS THEM IN POVERTY. They are paralyzed- they can't move. It's like being in bed trying to get up but you are so tired you can't move your body. So you just lie there and slowly fall asleep again. Then you wake up and the day is half over. You feel like a worthless slug. Meanwhile, the rich just made another 5 million and are jetting off to Paris for dinner.

Too many people overvalue what they are not and undervalue what they are.

Malcolm Forbes

Stop Blaming

The first thing you have to do is get over the victim mentality that you are poor because someone else made you that way. I know this goes against everything you are hearing, but if you want to become prosperous, you CANNOT think like a victim anymore. Stop blaming the government, the banks, the illuminati, the housing market, your boss, your spouse, your kids, your mortgage, your neighbor, your astrological sign, the sun, moon, the year, the stars, the time of the month, your friends, your parents, your childhood, your past lives, your stock broker, your body, your health condition, God, or anything else. It doesn't matter if they actually ARE trying to suppress you or not, you can overrule their energy with yours. If there are world conspiracies or not, it doesn't matter. Just remember this- TRUTH ALWAYS WINS. Always. Look at what happened to the Nazis and Communist Russia. When the world gets together to help the common good, it cannot be stopped. So what if there really is a world government illuminati attempt to rule the world? It is a lower energy, as compared to the higher frequency of all things good. It is your DUTY to become rich and powerful, except this time, you will use that power for good (right?). Either way, no matter what, you need to get over the whiny helpless victim thing and start claiming some serious power.

Taming the Monster

Your mind is an immature spoiled brat. It is a whiney selfish child throwing temper tantrums. It never got a proper education on how to behave itself. All it was raised on was random bits of miscellaneous sound bytes and media hype. It has no idea what reality is. It makes irrational decisions based on only what feels good right now. It's been taught to fear pretty much everything and trust nothing. It loves sugary stuff and scary stories, and thinks many of them are real.

And you are giving this thing the power to run your life ???

If you want a cohesive functional, productive successful life, you need to teach that brat some manners and train it to behave!

Have you ever noticed how most random thoughts you have are negative? Like some little trouble-maker inside seeing what it can get away with... seeing how many ways it can mess up your life, make you paranoid, play with you, warp your reality and drive you and everyone around you crazy.

Just like an uncontrollable child, when you catch it trying to poison your thoughts- STOP IT and correct it. Replace that negative thought with a positive one. It's time for some life-changing discipline.

A good way to motivate you is knowing that every negative thought COSTS YOU money, time, happiness, success, health, and chips away at your longevity and life itself. Every negative thought is a drop of poison. So when you catch one in the act, stop it immediately, rip it out and replace it with something constructive and positive. Negative thoughts take your power away. You need to put your foot down and claim your authority. Show your mind who's boss. Claim your power and tell it how you are not taking anymore shit from it. Shut up and play right, the truth is in charge now! Start filling up with as many empowering things as you can. Listen to powerful inspirational music, read empowering books, watch empowering videos, hang around empowering people and get yourself away from negative people as fast as you can and stay away. Your mind needs to be retrained fast and hard.

I am not talking about fluffy, positive mantras and affirmations. You can say all the flowery new-age stuff you want, but underneath, your subconscious is just laughing at you, knowing you are only trying to convince yourself, and it's not working. If you're into repetitive patterning, read this book over and over and over until it's ingrained in your being and you start doing this stuff without even thinking. I highly recommend this.

You need to quiet that annoying disbelieving mind that keeps spoiling and sabotaging great opportunities and relationships.

You need to start filling up with hardcore truth- stuff that you know is real. Never build your core on what other people say. Most of that is just theories. Build your base on what you personally know is real and keep your inner self as simple, clean and basic as possible. Do not try to memorize all kinds of studies, facts and statistics. Just get in touch with common sense. If I sense my mind getting cluttered, I do a brain dump- I throw it all out until there is just the basic instinct left of a cat. You know- a simple, quiet animal that just wants to eat, sleep, be loved, and quietly explore the world. If you think too much, you are polluting yourself and the world.

Rule your mind or it will rule you. – Horace

The Hurt Ego- "The Victim"

Many people who are in a non-supportive relationship try to prove to the other that it's their fault they failed or didn't become a success ("See? this is YOUR fault ... Just like I said ... Are you happy now?"). They purposely fail just to make a point- so the other person can feel bad. This is insane, selfish and very destructive all around. Nothing good ever comes of this and it's cruel. This is self-sabotaging behavior and a big waste of energy and time. Plus it ruins relationships. If you do this to someone else, it will come back and bite you in the ass. Do NOT expect this to lead to any kind of satisfaction. This kind of petty squabbling will only leave you in the gutter, broke and unhappy.

The only thing that will get you out is forgiveness, a clear peaceful mind and the positive energy of appreciation. You need some serious spring cleaning in your life, your home and your mind.

Everything is Mirrored Energy

You can't cheat the Universe (God) It knows your true intentions. What you put out comes back. You MUST do things from the goodness of your heart.

One of the rules of life is to give 10% of what you make to your favorite charity (those less fortunate). This is universal law. Even if you only have 10 cents, give one penny to your favorite cause. If that dime truly is everything you own, and you give away a penny to help someone else, the Universe will be so touched, it will help you more than you can imagine.

It's all about flow of energy. Life is movement. It flows. If the blood in your veins stops flowing, you die. If your breathing stops going in and out, you die. If your money doesn't flow, you go broke. I'm not saying to simply go out and buy stuff or give it away, that's foolish. Most poor people don't know how to spend their money wisely. They usually blow it on short-term instant gratification stuff. (Cigarettes, alcohol, junk food, drugs, cars, barbeques or whatever's on sale that week anywhere in town). I will talk more about how to divide up your money later (even if you have almost none).

Right now let's talk about energy. Money is energy. That's all it is. It's not good or bad. Just like a fork- you can use it to eat with, or as a weapon. It's not the tool, it's what you do with it. Money is just a tool, a benign piece of paper.

So, to recap- everything is energy and it needs to keep moving. It also comes back to you. What you put out comes back.

This is important. For example, when you tip someone for their services, don't tip begrudgingly or out of obligation, because the Universe will give you back begrudgingly... so in effect, <u>when you tip- you are tipping YOURSELF</u> !!!

I can't stress this enough. When you "donate" or "tithe" 10 percent of your income, you are giving to yourself. You can't see it, but somehow on a deeper level, you can feel it. If you expect the Universe to gift you millions, then you better prove you are worth it as a human being! Believe it or not, you'd be surprised how many of those mean, nasty rich people you hate secretly help others when no one is looking. Even a mafia guy would save a child from being hit by a car or has a grandmother they help. Don't ever judge or assume, because you are only condemning yourself. Negative thoughts are poison to prosperity. Stop poisoning yourself. Besides, it would be energy better spent to think about how you will thrive, rather than waste it thinking negative thoughts about others or feeling sorry for yourself. Get over it and start being constructive.

Try not to become a man of success, but rather try to become a man of value.

Albert Einstein

The greatest gift by the way is not money. It's you.

Be Careful Investing in Victims

Be careful. There are many people who are so caught in the victim mode feeling sorry for themselves, and nothing you do will help them, because they just want to prove to you and themselves that they are victims and the world is mean. They want you to cry for them. This is a form of attention they feed off. I sent a friend $400 as a gift, and right as they got it, their car suddenly needed $400 worth of work. It wouldn't have mattered if I gave them $4,000 or $40,000, that money would have been sucked out of their lives immediately. I see this pattern all the time. In another situation, I know someone who just made $5,000, and then almost immediately lost it all in a scam. If someone is in victim mode, they are putting a message out to the Universe *"please take my money from me so people will feel sorry for me and then maybe they'll give me even more money out of pity"*. It's a strange warped thinking, but it's the poor man's way of "investing". They think by having 900 dollars taken away from them will make some angel feel sorry and give them $9,000. It actually happens sometimes, but you know what happens then? Their inner programming can't stop (just like a drug addict)... if they got that $9,000, something would manifest that would take that from them also. So now they are thinking deep inside that maybe now the Universe will send an angel with $90,000! It could manifest as a possible pie-in-the-sky lawsuit payoff or inheritance, and it can get you all excited, but it never happens. This pattern is very common. I see it all the time and it's very sad. You could give them this book and they would refuse to believe it because they are stuck in their addictive pattern of having others enable them.

If any of you come asking me for money to invest in your ideas and projects, then you haven't learned a thing in this book. I am here to self empower you, not enable you. I can give you a fish and you'll eat it. The next day you're hungry again, asking me for another fish. I am teaching you how to fish here so you are in charge of your own life and you can go anywhere, anytime, and do anything. You will be totally portable and free. You won't need me or anybody to help you. The biggest problem with the United States is everybody depends on people outside of themselves for help. They depend on doctors to fix them after their bodies became run down from eating processed dead food. They depend on someone else for money. They depend on friends and spouse for emotional support. They depend on the media to tell them what's hot and what's not. They depend on banks and credit card companies to loan them money they don't have and didn't earn. The list goes on. If you shut down all grocery stores, restaurants, electricity and utilities, people would have no clue what to do. Absolutely none. They would probably start stealing from others, not knowing that the weeds and wild plants in their yard are edible and powerful medicine.

People are totally dependent on others for almost everything. This is a recipe for disaster. Then if something happens, what do they do? They blame others for their problems ...the government, banks, doctors, insurance companies etc, etc. Its always someone else's fault. Poor victims. Come on, grow up.

The "poor me" crybaby victim mentality needs to stop.

Give Up

Something needs to snap one day and they totally give up. Letting go is the best thing that could happen in this case. They need to just blank out and start over like a child, and see the wonder of a butterfly, the beauty of a flower, forgetting all of their issues and concerns. This may seem irresponsible to some, but that's the temporary phase they have to go through in order to reboot their operating system. A complete reprogramming of their hard drive.

Letting go to the truth is the only way.

For all of us.

"If you want to transform your health, start by transforming your thoughts."

Dr. Noah McKay MD "Wellness at Warp Speed"

Einstein's famous equation E=mc2 proved that matter and energy are the same. Energy manifests into matter and vice versa.

If you want to know what kind of energy your thoughts are creating, just look at your life. Look around you. You brought this to yourself. Does me saying that upset you? Then you are in victim mode. Take any great teaching... Jesus for example said *"Your faith is what healed you, not me"*. Did you hear that? He admitted he didn't do it. It was the person that did it to themselves. Yet countless people all over the world sit around waiting to be "saved". Folks, it's not going to happen if you don't get off your ass and change your energy, thoughts and actions right now!

Just get it into your thick head- no matter how much you lose, you never lose yourself. The rich know this, and that's what gives them the strength and freedom to do what they want. They don't care if they lose everything because anytime a hole is created, the universe fills it up with something else, usually newer and better.

I will say this stuff over and over again until it rings in your head like a song with an endless chorus.

Your emotions are not just internal. Their energy ripples out in waves and affects everything in your life. Everything. Like echo waves, they reflect back to you in the form of your future. So look around. Whatever is happening right now in your life is an echo of what emotions you sent out a little while back. How fast things come back to you depends on your emotional state. The more stagnant you are, the longer it drags out. The more you dwell on a painful past, the more you are strengthening and recreating it. People who stop dwelling on the past and stop talking about their "dis-ease" notice almost immediate and radical improvements in their lives.

For every action you put out, there are just as many equal reactions. This is universal law. This is what you call Life. Let me say that again- the energy you generate creates your life. What are you generating? Anger? Fear? or happiness and peace?

Remember what I said about giving. When you give to others, you are giving to yourself. So whatever you ask for in life, that's what you should be GIVING. I know it sounds strange, but that's how it works.

The intention is everything.

Do it with Love or don't do it

It may sound too easy for you, but do it- just start believing that everything is ok. Take a deep breath, relax and just keep telling yourself ... everything is o.k. Guess what? IT WORKS !!! Your subconscious doesn't know the difference. Whatever you believe, becomes your reality. It defies logic, but has been scientifically proven. Quantum physics and the field of epigenetics has won several Nobel prizes in this area.

What we Think, becomes Reality

*Whether you think you can
or you think you can't,
you're right.*

Henry Ford

Energy cannot be created of destroyed- it just changes form.
You have the power to change your life and your destiny.

The great thing about this, is it doesn't cost you ANYTHING !

There is nothing in the modern world that can match this level
of success, efficiency and power.

I will say this a million times- learning to let go of fear and
jumping into the unknown can save your life.

Common sense = if you are not well ... CHANGE !!!!!!!

When you are caught in a rut, you are doing the same mundane
lifeless things every day, and you are probably dwelling in self
pity and the past.

*Yesterday is a cancelled check; Tomorrow
is a promissory note; Today is the only
cash you have, so spend it wisely.*

Kim Lyons

Change

Change brings freshness into your life like nothing else. It wakes you up and puts you back into living in the moment.

Start with the small stuff you know you can handle

-turn off the TV

-surround yourself with beautiful things

-play beautiful music, sing, dance

-scream as loud as you want when no one is around

-run, hop up and down. Work out. Go to the gym

-do enemas

-learn jokes and tell them to people for no reason

-hug people, tell them you appreciate them

-give gifts- anything- even if it's just a token. Start getting rid of stuff.

You need to get the energy moving in your life!

World Economies

The misfortune of the wise is better than the prosperity of the fool. Epicurus

As I write this, the economies of America and Europe are teetering on the brink of collapse. Something cannot stay on top forever. Rome collapsed when it became too big, greedy, lazy and fat. It's part of natural life cycles for things to rise and collapse. Again, this is part of movement and flow. Nothing can stay the same forever. But don't worry. Economies rise and collapse all the time. It doesn't mean you will die. It doesn't mean you will starve. Houses will not vanish. It will just be a reshuffling of priorities, which is healthy. Change is needed to stir things up. Change is good and rich people know this. The richest people in the world became rich during hard times because they saw opportunity in change. The world is rich with opportunity right now. It's musical chairs time. Grab a chair. Every time there is change in anything, someone gets rich!

What do you have to offer the world? You will be paid according to the value of what you bring to the table. China and India figured out how to give us value. Now it's your turn.

We need to step back a bit and look at the bigger picture. In case you aren't aware of it yet, the whole world is NOT going through hard times. As a matter of fact, half the world is doing better than ever. China and India are producing millionaires by the minute. Their economies are stellar.

What was that? Did you feel a flash of bitterness, jealousy or resentment? You didn't want to hear that did you? You don't care about them do you? You just want YOU to be rich and forget everyone else. If you had ANY of these emotions, throw them out the window RIGHT NOW. They are poisoning your future. That negativity will bounce right back and send bitterness and ill feeling back to you. Stop it!

You need to wish them well, no mater who they are.

That is the only way to peace and prosperity.

Now, putting tyrannical governments aside, I know many "normal" Chinese people and they are wonderful. I spent a month in India and found them to be amazingly special highly spiritual souls. Some of my best friends are from India. I love their energy. They DESERVE to be prosperous. They are family. We are all connected. Help them and you will be helped back.

IMPORTANT- Do NOT do something with the expectation of getting something back. The Universe can see right through that selfish intention. Remember- intention is everything. If you give expecting to get back, then people will do the same to you.

Give out of the goodness of your heart. Enjoy the act of giving, even if it is just loving thoughts, prayers and well wishes. It's all powerful energy.

Don't whine, resist or argue with reality.

Become the reality you want.

You change your life by changing the quality of this moment.

Speaking of everything being energy, be aware that places have energy also. Have you ever walked into a place and instantly felt creeped out? Or felt really excited? There is positive and negative energy everywhere. You need to be aware of this, and it can strongly influence your life in every way.

The Chinese put great importance on Feng Shui, the science of energy in your home- which way it is facing, the layout of the rooms, the objects in the rooms, colors, vibrations etc. It all affects you, your moods, success and ability to thrive. There must be something to it all because the Chinese are taking over the world (and I don't mean that in a bad way). Even communism becomes a temporary hiccup. It cannot last. Stop fearing change. When Rome took over the barbaric countries, it brought massive class and culture upgrades to those cultures. We all have a lot to learn from each other. It is inevitable that everything eventually melts together.

Resistance is futile. It is death. (and a great waste of energy)

Flowing, accepting and adapting is life.

We are entering an era where everyone must work together. Our consciousness has already started melting into one. Thanks to the internet, communication is becoming instant. This is the most exciting time in human history and we are right in the middle of being reborn into a new world. Just think of the new power and advancements when everyone on the planet puts their heads and hearts together and starts creating something seven billion times stronger than if we did something on our own. We are not losing our personal identity, but gaining the best of everyone else on the planet. We have unlimited power now.

Don't worry about success. It already exists. All you have to do is allow it. Shut up and get out of the way of your thoughts. Open the door and let success in. It's been knocking on your door from the moment you were born, but you kept ignoring it, thinking you know better. You thought you knew what job was right for you (or maybe you just guessed). And look where you are now. So are you ready to finally relax for a minute and let the experts come in and give your life a serious makeover?

Others are hopping on the band wagon. The party has already started. Don't miss it. It's way better and more fun than your little pity party. Life is too short to waste on negative stuff and revenge and regrets. Stop thinking so much and start living NOW!

Stop copying others

Create your own Trend

The moment something new and big comes out, others try to copy that formula. But they will never be the first big one. So stop thinking you need to make another_____ because _____ is doing it and they are successful. You are NOT them! You are YOU. What do YOU have to offer the world that no one else has? What makes YOU unique? THAT is your ticket to success. Have the courage to wager everything you have on yourself. The more unique you are, the more your value increases. There is only one of you in the world. So what is unique about you?

Whatever you do- DO IT WELL, from the heart.

Be the best at what you do, and get it out to as many people as possible.

"You never change things by fighting the existing reality. To change something, build a new model that makes the existing model obsolete."

Buckminster Fuller

Stuart Wilde said it best;

"The key to success is to raise your own energy: when you do, people will naturally be attracted to you."

What you cannot see is infinitely more powerful than anything you can see.

Change the Cause, not the Symptom

Whatever you see in the physical world is the result of something that was first energetically created. Money is just a symptom. Just like I wrote in my health book- cancer, diabetes, heart disease etc, are just symptoms. To not have the problem anymore, don't just remove the symptom (cancer), you need to STOP DOING WHAT CAUSED IT in the first place!

You can't simply cut the cancer out and keep smoking, drinking, eating pork rinds and potato chips.

The same goes for money and prosperity. Those are just symptoms of someone who's got the right energy. You can't simply go after the money while still being messed up in the head energetically.

That's why poor people who win lotteries almost always end up losing the money again, while rich people keep making money back, even if they lose it all.

The higher your energy vibration, (in other words, the more positive it is) ...the more prosperity will attract to you. If you are a shining beacon of light, things will naturally attract your way like bugs to a lantern. But if you are a miserable bottomless pit of despair with nothing but sob stories about how unlucky you are, ...do you think people want to hang around? Do you think anything wants to be near that? That's negative energy and it pushes things, people and prosperity away.

I have seen people in the hardest times still keep an up attitude no matter what. They were the first ones out of the hole, like they were snatched by angels. The rest still wallowed in darkness and fell even deeper into depression because they blamed the "lucky" ones with having favoritism from the universe. They are right. The Universe favors positive energy.

People are so obsessed with results. They want to jump right to the end- money, sex, power, good looks, big house, social status, etc. and they will take whatever shortcuts they can afford.

There are no shortcuts. People spend more time and energy looking for shortcuts than if they actually did it right in the first place. And shortcuts are temporary fixes usually of a much lower quality than the real thing. Ultimately the real thing would have cost less, been less hassle and been a lot more stable and long lasting. We need to realize, there ARE no such things as shortcuts. They are temptations that distract us.

As a matter of fact, shortcuts usually cause damage and take longer to backtrack and repair. You don't get younger by having plastic surgery. You get younger by deep cleaning your body and rebuilding your liver, kidneys, colon and outlook on life. People go to skin centers to have their face pulled, lasered, stitched, sucked and injected and they start looking like freaks. That's why I wrote the book "HEAL YOUR FACE", because people had no clue that wrinkles and lines on the face were merely symptoms (that can be reversed). But the only way to do this is a serious life change- your face is a mirror of your health. Every part of your face is connected to a different body part. For example, if you have frown lines and crows feet, that means your liver is toxic. If you have bags or wrinkles under you eyes, that's a kidney issue. If you have deep grooves running from your nose to the sides of your mouth (nasolabial folds), that means you have colon problems.

Yes they can be reversed. How much depends on how serious you are in cleaning and LETTING GO of your destructive habits. And I can guarantee you, 90 percent of people don't want to do what it takes. They want to take the easy road or comfort and convenience. So they will never get younger (or prosperous)

Again, there are no real shortcuts. Sure you can get plastic surgery and you might look good for a while, but underneath you are still rotting away, until one day you have colon, kidney or liver cancer. Most people at this point act surprised and start with the "poor me" victim mode. Must be poor genetics (blame the parents), must be all those GMO foods (blame industry), must be stress (blame spouse or bills), must be toxic workplace (blame job). Come on people. Take some responsibility in your life. Science has proven you can change your genetics within SECONDS just by the way you think. That's right, you can turn genes on and off simply with the energy of your thoughts and emotions. If you don't believe me, look it up. Read the book "The Genie in your Genes". Several Nobel prizes have been won on the subject. Your mind and emotions have the power to literally change your life.

The point is, cancer etc, is just a symptom and life was warning you a long time before it showed up. Your face is like the dash of your car- it has warning lights and gauges all over it. You just have to learn what they mean, and NOT hide them with surgery because they are there to help you. If you get rid of the cause, the warning lights (wrinkles, lines, bumps, spots, warts, moles, thinning hair, grey hair etc) go away again. That's why I wrote the book "Heal Your Face". Stop treating the symptoms and deal with the CAUSE !

If you want prosperity, success, money and happiness, and you don't have any of that right now, you can't keep doing the same things you have been doing and expect different results. You need to change YOU.

If things aren't going well in your life (your outer reality), then things are not running smoothly inside your head and spirit, because the outside is just a reflection of how well you're doing inside energetically. Those outside things are your warning lights. Pay attention.

Commit

Here is an easy thing to do. State your commitment out loud in front of other people. You'll be amazed how powerful this is. Why? Because like I said earlier, we care what other people think about us. We are a vain species. We don't want to look like fools in front of other people. So when we state a commitment out loud in front of others (the more people, the better), the more we have to follow through, stick to it and make it happen, otherwise we look like fools.

So figure out what your goals are (not just "make a lot of money") and make it official out loud in public. You will be amazed how much you'll get done when your reputation is on the line!

Do it for the Right Reason

Intention is everything. The Universe is watching. Before you start, be careful and aware of WHY you want money and success. Is it because you feel the need to "prove" yourself? Is it because you fear poverty and want to stockpile? Be careful. Do it for the right reasons or you will not be happy. You MUST be true to yourself and the Universe. You are playing with powerful stuff here, and the last thing you want after a lifetime of stress is another hard painful lesson.

You don't need big expensive things to feel good. Remember, you should be happy if you have very little or a lot, it shouldn't matter. Money does not guarantee happiness. Stuff comes and goes. What is the real reason you want money and success? To have no more bills and stress? Rich people have bills too. There will always be challenges and stressful tests. That never goes away.

This is a serious question. One that determines the quality of your future.

It's not hard to make decisions when you know what your values are. Roy Disney

If you get more money, you'll probably just get bigger, more expensive things... which leads to more bills and stress, which leads to the next lesson ...

MONEY IS NOT SECURITY

This is the biggest illusion you could have about money. Security doesn't exist. It is a fear-based concept. Even if you made a lot of money, you would probably then fear losing it. So now you need security for your security. Money comes and goes. Even the richest people go bankrupt many times over. Their security is not the money- it's knowing they can make it back again.

The ONLY security you will ever really have is inner peace with yourself. Integrity is the only real security. It has nothing to do with money whatsoever. You know deep inside that this life is all just a video game. Money, people, houses, jobs etc, all come and go. Even Donald Trump has been bankrupt multiple times. None of it matters. As long as you have inner peace you are ok.

There is no security on this earth, there is only opportunity.
General Douglas MacArthur

What are you really worried about? We have already established that you can't starve. Are you worried that if you go broke your lover will leave you? If they do, they weren't with you for the right reasons anyway. True relationships last no matter what. They see life as an adventure. A true mate would go "Hey, if we have to camp in a tent for a while, so be it. It's kinda cool to reconnect with nature anyway". Life is a rollercoaster and rollercoasters are supposed to be a thrill. Nothing stays the same forever. It's putting your hands in the air and going "Woohoooo" and taking it all in stride that can turn something seemingly bad into something wonderful. Many people pay money to go camping. Many grocery stores are now selling dandelion greens. A few years ago, people would have went "Ewww, I have to eat weeds?" Now they pay good money for these exotic salads at fancy restaurants. It's all a matter of perspective.

In order to succeed, your desire for success should be greater than your fear of failure.

Bill Cosby

Money and Relationships

The biggest cause of breakups in relationships is money. This is so sad. Two beautiful loving souls being torn apart because of some paper and numbers that a few years from now will mean nothing. It's not really about how much money they have, but how it's spent. Odds are, each person has a different idea of how it should be used. The reason for this is each person was raised differently with different programming. Usually these differences clash somehow because no two people are the same, or at least cause some sort of fear in one or both. The answer is not simply making more money (which could lead to burnout and resentment), but dealing with the core issues, namely the programming. This takes honesty and calm open talk without becoming upset or heated. Both people need to be receptive and understanding of the other's upbringing and belief system.

Both need to be flexible and willing to work with the other within reasonable agreed-upon boundaries. It needs to make sense.

It usually has to do with different priorities. One person might be fearful of hard times and try to save as much money as possible, while the other says we need to live a little, otherwise what's the use of living. Somewhere they have to meet in the middle, agree on a plan of some sort, and stick to it.

First, figure out your mutual goals. What do you have in common and agree upon? Start with the basics and work your way towards the details.

After reading this book, hopefully the fear factor will have been tamed somewhat. You DO need to live a little and have fun. And you DO need to be smart with your money. Balance is the key. The Universe could not exist without balance. For every force, there is an opposite and equal force. For every day, there is night. Yin /Yang. Man/Woman, Hot/Cold, Summer/ Winter.

Managing Your Money

Until now, the money has been controlling you. You need to start controlling your money.

Most people have no clue how to handle money. They make it and then they spend it. Somehow the "bills" seem to always equal the money coming in. There never seems to be any left. How does that happen?

It's actually quite simple, and there is an answer to that.

First of all, like I said earlier, any time a hole is made, the Universe will fill it. If you come home with 400 dollars, you will find $400 worth of bills. If you get $1500, you will figure out exactly how that $1500 gets broken up. If you made $10,000 , the same. If you luck out and get two million, you will go and buy a new house, a new car, new furniture and celebrate with a trip to Hawaii... the final cost- over 2 million ! There is no end to this. You will always find a way to spend that money, even if you were a Billionaire.

That's probably why the Universe isn't giving you millions of dollars... because you don't know how to handle it.

Let me help you become worthy.

This is what I do and it seems to work.

Step 1: <u>Know Where Your Money is Going</u>

Most people don't really have a grasp of where their money is going. What's a real eye opener is when you actually start keeping track. A big part of the problem is actually the little things. We don't pay much attention to them- we get a burrito on the way home, or hey, there's a sale at the mall, and look, here's a coupon for 25% off at _____. To really grab the monster by the horns, you have to know what you are dealing with. So from this moment on- ANY - and I mean ANY- money you and your spouse spend needs to be written down and recorded at the end of every day. Every tank of gas, every coffee latte, every car wash, every piece of chocolate, every DVD rental, every burrito, every spontaneous little thingy you grab as you run around every day. If you add up all the tiny simple little expenses (like one Starbucks coffee every day) compounded over years ultimately ends up costing you millions!

Once you see it listed on paper at the end of the day, (only takes a few minutes), you start grabbing control of your life again.

Step 2: <u>The Different Accounts</u>

This is important. The moment you get any money, it needs to be immediately divided into categories.

I opened six bank accounts and this is how I immediately divide the money...

SIX ACCOUNTS

1. Business   25%

2. Bills   25%

3. Taxes   25%

4. Give   10%

5. Savings   10%

6. Play   5%

1. Business.

This is the cost of running your business. Your business is your investment in yourself and your dreams of helping the world. Maybe you are not self-employed, so you won't have any big business expense. But I suggest you still keep your business money so you can start saving for your own business asap. If your taxes are taken out by your employer, then I suggest for the time being, you make your savings 20% and divide the rest between bills and business. Remember, rich people are self employed. Poor people work for others. If you have a weekly paycheck as an employee, start aiming for independence because employees almost never become rich and prosperous. They are slaves.

2. Bills

Most people have their bills (cost of living) being at least 50% of their income. Poor people are usually around 100%. (I'll explain why later). Maybe you need to start at 50%, but work on changing this down to 25%.

I simplified my life and got rid of expensive things so my cost of living was down to 25% of my income. This includes mortgage, food, utilities, etc. You are probably higher, so work on lowering your cost of living! Simplification is a universal law of increasing energy flow and success. Airplanes fly faster when they have less baggage. Lightweight race cars are faster. Hikers with very light backpacks can hike further and faster. When you have less baggage in life, you have less stress, move faster, and get things done more efficiently. You sleep better at night and live longer. It is the one common factor for all-around health that I also write about in my book Heal Yourself 101- cleaning out the crap from your life, body, mind and soul. There is a misconception that all rich people have lots of stuff and they waste money. Actually many rich people are very efficient and have very simple lives. Many of them simpler than yours. Have you ever noticed how rich people work very little and the poor people are slaving all day long? SIMPLIFY YOUR LIFE! Get your costs down, down, down! Donate, sell or throw out everything you possibly can. You are in a hot air ballon thats about to ram into a mountain. Dump your weight so you can rise above your problems. The lower your cost of living, the more power you have to get out of your hole.

3. Taxes

If you're self employed, it's better to save for taxes the minute you get money. Poor people don't save for taxes because they focus on immediate emergencies (many of which can be avoided if they change their negative energy thinking pattern and simplify their lives). If you are self-employed and have a lot of deductions, then you will have money left over at the end of the year in the tax account. This is a secondary backup source. Whatever's left, put it into the savings account and don't touch.

4. Give

One tenth of your income needs to be passed on to helping others. This is universal law. If you cheat here, life will cheat you. Remember, it's all energy, so you are actually investing positive energy in yourself. What you put out comes back. If you are doing this right, you should feel a rush every time you do this because you are doing a good deed. You can literally feel good energy immediately coming into your life. But don't do with any conscious expectations or getting something back.

You have not lived today until you have done something for someone who can never repay you. – John Bunyan

5. Savings

10% goes into savings and never gets touched no matter what. Do NOT have any weak moments. You can make almost any emergency work without touching this. The more positive and healthier your life is, the fewer emergencies you have anyway. So what do you use this for? Investing in things that go up in value. This way you will never lose money in this category. This is your cradle.

6. Play (10% if you want faster results)

Finally, 5% goes to the PLAY account and you need to spend this - do not hoard it and turn it into an emergency savings account. This 5% is for you to reward yourself and do things that feel good... get massages, go to a nice restaurant, take a road trip and stay in a fancy hotel etc. This is very important for several reasons. Remember, everything is energy and what you do and think becomes your reality. You need to start knowing what it feels like to be rich, successful and prosperous. Your mind needs to get used to the good life. This is subconscious success-programming and it's more important than you think. This is NOT frivolous self-indulgent spending in a time where you could use the money elsewhere. This is an investment in YOU and your FUTURE. If you are going to train someone to be a bus driver, they need to drive a bus for a while to get used to it. The same goes for prosperity. You need to get accustomed to what it feels like to be COMFORTABLE and stress-free in life... to feel good and be pampered. To have people take care of your needs instead of you constantly taking care of others. You MUST be comfortable with this energetically otherwise you will never allow true success.

Anybody who thinks they can't afford this category and says *"this is frivolous, we could use this money for bills"* will stay poor. You become rich by treating yourself like a rich person. If you feel you don't deserve it right now, you will stay right where you are and not step up in life. Becoming rich isn't about your money, it's about you and how you feel.

Simplify, Simplify, Simplify

Many of you will immediately say "But we don't have enough money to do that, we barely make enough to pay bills as it is". Firstly, that's a statement coming from someone who thinks they are a powerless victim with no control over their own life. Start taking control right now. The biggest battle you will ever fight is with your own personal programming. Stop convincing yourself there is no way out. If you have too many bills, then get a cheaper car or house, or make it a mission to go through everything in your life and make it more efficient. You don't need all that crap you own. You can radically cut your expenses if you put your mind to it.

Imagine an emergency where you knew your house was going to be destroyed and you only had six hours to get your most important things and leave. What would you take? Your passport, driver's license, some clothes, cell phone, laptop and back-up hard drive with all your important files and info. I would take my Vitamix blender of course, haha. This is how you need to think about what you really need in life. It's actually very little. If you are making payments on silly stuff like cable TV etc, that's a good place to start cutting. TV is a mind-rotting waste of precious time anyway. If you really put your mind to it, you can cut your bills down to 25%. This down-sizing is making room for the new things about to come into your life.

This multiple account money-management formula has worked for many, many people. Its helped get them out of the mess they are in. Its helped them not spend money prematurely in the wrong places. This really works. I used to always spend money when it came in and had nothing left by the end of the day. Everything changed when I started doing this. In a very short amount of time, you will see your life actually in control and money start to accumulate.

I don't want to hear any excuses. Do you want to become wealthy and prosperous or not? Roll up your sleeves and make this happen, whatever it takes. And do NOT have weak moments and steal from one category to pay for overspending in another.

Anyway, you get the idea. The moment you get any money- it immediately goes into these accounts. It's pretty easy nowadays because it's all done on computer via online banking. My income is basically all through Paypal which I transfer into the respective accounts before I can spend it and possibly get myself into trouble. This is money management and controls the spontaneous spending of the past when money came in.

The Difference

The difference between rich and poor is mindset. Rich people MAKE and INVEST money. Poor people SPEND money. The perspective needs to change and this management system is a simple way to start.

Becoming wealthy and prosperous requires some discipline, and this is a strong start. The problem with poor people is the minute they get money, they SPEND it. If they make more money, they get a better car. If they make even more, they get a bigger house. This never ends. The minute they get money, they spend it. It goes to their head. More clothes, bigger vacations, they want to feel they are moving up in the world. They get ten dollars, they spend ten dollars. They get ten thousand- they spend ten thousand. The problem is, they never have anything left, and this is NOT called prosperity. Having a bigger house means bigger house payments and working harder. You are a hamster in a wheel, running like crazy getting nowhere. At the end of the day, you say to yourself "I'm making more money, but have none left- where did it all go? I don't get it." Sound familiar? Probably. That's over 90% of the world. There isn't much thought in the process- it's all instant gratification, now, now, now, me, me, me. But the blame always goes to "them", (anybody "out there" that makes an easy blame target).

Many rich people started right where you are now- with very little. I personally started with nothing when I came back from the desert. The reason the rich became rich while most don't is because they were smart with their money. They simplified their lives down to the very minimum and used every penny wisely. If they only had 400 dollars and their car needed a 400 dollar repair, they would sell the car for 500 dollars, buy a motorcycle for 400 dollars and use the remaining 500 for their business. If they had a house, they got rid of it and moved temporarily into an apartment, because they knew they could buy any mansion in a short while. They looked down the road and invested in their goal like their life depended on it, because ultimately, it does.

But most people need an instant gratification fix just to make it through the day. Spending makes them feel good, like it helps prove they still have freedom. Nobody wants to feel trapped. But what they are really doing is giving away the very tool that could have dug them out of prison.

Because it's a mental addiction issue, this is the same problem people have with the health of their bodies- it's all about instant gratification- they eat food they know isn't good for them, but it tastes great. They think "what difference is this one pizza or cookie going to make?" But it never ends. Then they start aging, have trouble getting out of bed because their energy levels drop, their relationships suffer because they are irritable and have sexual performance issues, etc. They lose hair, get wrinkles and go to get plastic surgery to hide it, which is a joke.

Now if they just had a little discipline and said NO to the instant gratification, and started living like nature intended, all those problems would go away and they would thrive and prosper.

I'm explaining the health parallel with financial prosperity because the common factor in both is YOU and your knee-jerk reaction to what you eat and how you spend your money. Stop with the short term drug fix and start controlling yourself. You are in this for the long haul and if you want to prosper, you need to start being a new you, right now, before there are too many problems to fix.

Start with what you can handle.

Even if you only put a dime in each account each time- you must start somewhere. You must put one foot forward to start walking. After a while you will start to see money accumulating in the various accounts and you will start to get a little excited. This is positive energy and it will build. This will build momentum and before you know it, you will exponentially become prosperous.

Start controlling your unconscious urges right now. The moment you clean up your act and start doing the right thing, you feel a power inside you. You instantly feel cleaner, stronger and in control. The change can be instantaneous.

The Biggest Excuse

Poor people claim they don't have any money to manage, but one day, when they get it, then they will manage it. But right now, there is no extra money, so it's just survival mode. (is this you?) First of all, stop waiting for "extra" money. We are talking about what you have right now, no matter how small. You need to start somewhere, even if it's just a dime. Re-read the part I just wrote about downsizing to bare necessities.

Until now, the money has been controlling you. You need to start controlling your money. I will keep saying this.

The Universe (God) is watching you. It has unlimited power. It is your greatest (actually ONLY) investor, but it is a wise, shrewd investor. First you must prove you can handle a dime before it gives you a dollar. When you show you can handle a dollar, it will give you a hundred dollars... and so on.

If you just had an angry response like *"Of course I know how to handle money, how dare you!"*, then that means your ego has been activated. Rich people are always open to learning new tricks. They are receptive and listen well. Poor people think they know everything and are very stubborn and defensive. You can't receive when you are too busy exploding outwards. Remember, it's all energy. Start drawing energy TOWARDS you, not pushing it away. So whenever ANYONE gives you any feedback, no matter WHO they are- listen to them and really think about what the Universe is trying to tell you. Often times the Universe (truth) speaks to you through some of the strangest people and situations. It could even be someone you despise, but don't be fooled. The message is always around you being reflected by WHOEVER is conveniently here right now. People are your mirrors. They reflect you and what you need to learn. Even the most aggravating relationships can be your greatest teachers. Stop thinking everyone is crazy but you and that you are always right and nobody else knows what they are talking about. Get your silly ego out of the way. I am amazed every time I meet a super rich person, how quickly they are able to LISTEN and LEARN. Believe it or not, they know how to humble themselves on the spot and be receptive. Those are the TRUE rich people. Anyone who instinctively fights you and argues and says things without thinking is probably broke.

If you could kick the person in the pants responsible for most of your trouble, you wouldn't sit for a month. T. Roosevelt

OK, are you a little more open to listening and learning? Are you willing to try something new or are you going to resist and fight me on this?

I don't care how broke you are. I don't care how little you have. Even if it's a few dollars, it can be used to get you out of the hole you are in. Each situation is different. The first step is to WANT to get out of the hole. The second is to BELIEVE it's possible some how. The third is to get rid of everything that's irritating, distracting, burdening and keeping you down. SIMPLIFY your life. Downsize your money pit car and house if you must. Grow your own food. If you have to, remember you can eat weeds, and most plants in your neighborhood are edible. They can heal your health issues. Learn which ones are edible. Dandelions are a good start. Go online. The answers to your problems are always within reach. All you have to do is look around. The forth step is to clear away all the bad programming you have about money, success, prosperity and rich people. This is key or anything you make will be taken away again, leaving you where you started. The fifth step is to clear your life and your mind so you can figure out why you are here and what your mission is. You need to have a goal (it can't simply be becoming rich). What do you have that can help others?

> *If you're going to be thinking,*
> *you may as well think big.*
>
> Donald Trump

The sixth step is to take what you have and use every penny, every drop, every ounce to make your thing happen. It must be planned out like a great military strike. Every penny is a soldier ready to go to battle for you. They are awaiting your commands. Be smart. Don't let them die in vain. Protect them, honor them. They are your future.

The only one in control of your life is YOU.

This is God's gift to you... freedom to make your own choices.

Make good choices. The Universe is watching. You will be rewarded.

Defeat is not the worst of failures. Not to have tried is the true failure.
George Edward Woodberry

Remember, you have 5-10 percent set aside for pampering yourself, so it's not all work and no play. You need to get used to thinking rich. This means getting used to RECEIVING, not just giving.

The Key: Your Programming

This is the most important factor of all. Your programming determines what kind of energy you put out, which determines what (and who) you attract, push away and what your limits are. Even if you were fearless, you will always end up with what you are programmed for. Let's say your programming has you comfortable with 100 thousand a year. No matter how hard you try, you will always end up with just that amount, because that's your comfort level. Even if you made 200 thousand, you would energetically attract something that would make you lose 100 of it, or you'd have a bad year after that to make up the difference. It works in reverse also. If you have a bad year, you will have a good year soon after that to make up for it.

After a while, you will feel comfortable with that 100 thousand and have this suspicion you will always be taken care of, no matter what. And you are right- you ARE taken care of... by YOU! ...by your programming that you allowed to form and run your life at a level you are "realistically" comfortable with.

Your secret inner belief system is what creates your world.

No matter what your dreams or hopes are on the outside (wishes), it's your inner belief system (your programming) that determines the outcome, because in your subconscious, you are saying "I would like_____, but realistically, I will probably just get_____." And so it is.

You get what you expect.

It's that simple.

If you are a woman who grew up in a family or society where women make very little, you will expect that, so you'll probably end up with a man that also makes very little or can't handle money well to make your expectations come true. Wishes and hopes don't makes things happen, expectations do.

Likewise, if you are a man that's programmed to only make a certain amount and no more, you will bring into your life a woman that loves spending, so even if you made lots of money, she will keep you at your original level and spend the rest.

This is a big cause of frustration, arguments and breakups, but it's each person's <u>programming</u> causing it. This needs to be cleaned up and upgraded.

You see the same patterns in people all the time.

- Some people can never hold a job for a long time.

- Some people make lots of money, no matter what

- Some people make only a certain amount, no matter how hard they try

- Some people make good money, only to lose it right away once they make it.

- Some people meet big money investors and everything looks great but nothing ever happens, over and over and over

Do you have a pattern that happens consistently your whole life and you wonder why? Do you feel like you are jinxed? Like some karmic spell has been put on you?

That "spell" is the accumulation of all the beliefs you heard and picked up early in your life. If your parents worked really hard but made very little, chances are you are doing the same.

If a woman's parents divorced when she was a child and she watched her mother struggle, the woman will probably not trust that men will take care of her, and that relationships probably won't last, so she'll sabotage every relationship she ends up in, and possibly also any money between the two, because struggle is all she knows and is comfortable with.

The stories are endless, and most people's repeating patterns can almost always be traced back to something in the formative early years of life.

It will keep happening unless you change your inner programming. Just like the "victim" mentality, you are constantly validating your inner belief system programming. If you see something happening over and over, you start to expect it to continue happening. You actually start looking for it to prove you are on to something. And guess what? What you seek, you shall find.

This is one of the biggest most perplexing frustrations people have- they see the same patterns happening over and over in their lives with money, relationships, health, you name it. Your programming determines almost everything. This is common sense. What we observe as children becomes our reality. If we see people struggling, we think life is a struggle. If we grow up in Beverly Hills, we think life is easy and no matter what we do, money will always flow, no matter how much we blow money, there will always be more. The same in relationships- you will keep finding people with the same problems and traits, no matter how many people you go through. Many people say "ok, I've learned my lesson, ok that will never happen again!" Yes it will, even if you learned your lessen. If you are programmed to be a certain way, then you will always end up that way.

Unless you change your programming.

If you want your money to grow, then YOU need to grow.

If you want your relationship to improve, it's trickier because YOU might improve your programming, but it doesn't mean the other person will. If you suddenly acquire a millionaire's mindset, but your mate still has a spending issue, you are in for quite a ride. There is no guarantee two people will change at the same time.

"Business is simple. People are complicated"

T. Harv Eker

How to Change

The first step is to realize what's going on.

Then you need to recognize the pattern.

Then you need to figure out where it came from.

Once you see the trail, you can step back like a detective and go "Aha! I see now. Wow, how silly of me to still believe this crap." Once you see something for what it is, you have instantly begun the transformation of taking its power away. You've had a parasite quietly living inside you , sucking you of your life force. No matter how much "food" and money you put into your life, the parasite will eat more and more of it, getting bigger, fatter and stronger inside you, while you become more tired, frustrated and run down on the outside, wondering where all the money goes, or food, or time, or...

But once you look inside and SEE the parasite, you can get rid of it. Those old fashioned beliefs are your parasite.

You might look inside and realize one of your beliefs is "rich people are bad". Exposing it is one thing, but do you believe it? Do you still have a little doubt that this might be actually true? If so, you need to work on that. You can't just say it's not true, you have to actually believe it in your heart. Do what you must to dispel those myths. This can get a little tricky because remember- you will always prove you are right, no matter what side you are on. If you believe rich people are bad, you will find bad rich people to prove it. What you must understand is there is always another side to the coin- there are also nice rich people- and you can become one of them. Or let's say there are NO nice rich people- ... if you really had the courage to do so, you could be the first ever nice rich person! You see, just because everyone else is a certain way, doesn't mean you can't be the first at something. Those are the people that make history.

Back in the 1400's, the belief was still that the world was flat and if you went far enough, your ship would fall off the edge. People actually believed this! So sailors didn't go very far- they always stayed close to land. One day, a now-famous guy said "You know what? I don't think so" and the rest is history.

A successful man is one who can lay a firm foundation with the bricks others have thrown at him. David Brinkley

Prove to the world it isn't flat and suddenly it's round. Prove to yourself being rich isn't bad and suddenly you are rich. Go out there and meet lots of rich people- discover the new world.

Successful People do Homework

Poor people think they know everything. Rich people know there is always more to learn. If there is pain in life, the first thing I want to do is find out what's causing it (not hide it) and then make it my priority to get rid of the source of my pain- no matter how much homework, research, trial and error it took. Thomas Edison went through a thousand different materials before he found a light bulb filament that worked. Everybody in the scientific community laughed at him until then. The only thing I believe is what actually works, not what others say.

Are you one of those people strong enough to break the belief system and prove everyone wrong? Are you strong enough to stand up against the whole world and follow your heart, no matter what others tell you or think about you?

There are those of us (me included) who don't give a rat's ass (excuse my French) about chem-trails, illuminati, communistic takeovers, Nazis, new world order, Monsanto, evil bankers etc etc, etc. I am not saying none of that is true, but the people that worry about that stuff will attract that to their lives and be very unhappy. I for one am here to get on with my life and live it as fully as I can while I am here. I want to feel the sun on my face and make love every chance possible. I want to make music, movies, write books and travel. I want to lie on a tropical beach naked and embrace all life everywhere. My job is to inspire the world and by God I am going to do that no matter what!

You create your own reality. Quantum physics has proved it. You can change anything and everything RIGHT NOW by what you think, feel, believe and put energy into.

Here is an email I recently received from Swami Ramananda Maharaj

"People are very scared, some say it's the illuminati, others feel we are on the verge of revolution, one person today insisted I leave the country.....they are all asking me to look into the future, I told them "to look at this moment, NOW. Conscious living in this moment determines the future. If we focus on this moment NOW and all its positive potential, we can bring enlightenment to our world, we can bring Light to the negativity of fear that only immobilizes us, and Most importantly I believe that we can change the world with ONE powerful thought." It's time to believe, I do not plan to leave the country soon, this is where my work is.   Much love, Swami"

I choose to be in a romance movie. If you want to be in a horror drama, then you are free to do so, but I'll be in the theater next door having the time of my life, because I've been given the greatest gift imaginable- to be in a human body so God can feel through my body what it's like to feel, see, smell, touch, taste all the beauty and wonders of nature and another human being. I get chills from even the simplest things like the sound of someone quietly turning the page of a book in a silent room, or the sound of fingertips quietly dancing on a keyboard nearby. I love the sound of my lover's breath as she peacefully sleeps inches away. I love how amazing, soft and warm human skin feels and how I can see the entire universe in someone's eyes.We are here to APPRECIATE life, not fear it! And the sooner you realize that, the sooner you start to really live.

Get over all your guilt.

You can't help the poor when you yourself are poor.

It's ok to fly in a private jet and have millions of dollars. It's ok to be rich. It's ok to have nice clothes. There will ALWAYS be poor people in the world. You can't help them all. Even if you gave them money, they would probably blow it. I've tried it and that's exactly what happened over and over. You need to teach them to self empower themselves.

There will always be bad people. That's their role in this movie. Every film needs a bad guy. If it wasn't for the darkness, you couldn't see the stars. Your job is to be the star in your own movie. Start acting like one! The world needs heroes. People need someone to look up to. Don't be poor just because there are other poor people out there. They need a hero. And the more power and money you get, the more you can help them. Power attracts power. The Universe will give you whatever you need to get the job done. If you can get more done by being in three cities in one day without waiting in lines at airports, then a private jet makes sense. The days are rushing by and we have lots of important things to do in a short amount of time. The world needs us, badly. Let's shine and raise the vibration of this planet like never before. Prosperity and happiness is our birthright. It is not something to be embarrassed about or feel guilty over. Be the sexiest, richest, happiest, best, loving, giving, beautiful prosperous person you can be.

Notice I had the word "giving" in there. That is the magic ingredient. It's what helps attract more prosperity to your life (give and ye shall receive). It also clears you of the guilt trip. It's ok to be super rich, as long as you give some of it back. All living things in nature give back what they take. It's the natural design. Nature holds the patterns for success. All we have to do is learn from nature and get back to the truth.

Success will not lower its standard to us. We must raise our standard to success.

Rev. Randall R. McBride, Jr.

The Truth

The truth is your guide. If you ever get lost or confused in life, simplify and connect with the truth, because the truth will always set you free. If life gets too complicated... get back to what you know is the truth.

As for all the conspiracy theories, I don't care if they are true or not, because evil never lasts. It can't. Evil is Live spelled backwards. It is the reverse of living. History proves over and over that tyranny cannot prevail, because it is not based on truth. There are only two things in the Universe- Love and Fear. Love is the truth, and fear is not knowing the truth. Mean people are mean because of fear. They don't know the truth. Just remember, no matter what happens, things will always work out in the end (in the long run).

Gandhi said it best...

"Whenever I despair, I remember that the way of truth and love has always won. There may be tyrants and murderers, and for a time, they may seem invincible, but in the end, they always fail. Think of it: always."

They can torture your body, your bank account and take all your belongings and even your life, but they can never take the freedom of your soul.

Always remember that. You are a free being and always will be.

Start living like one.

When you are ok with losing everything, is when you finally "get" everything.

You GET, when you "get it".

Get it?

The secret is to not need anything. Needy people don't get anything because they can't appreciate what they have. The Universe will give you everything you need when you are ready. You will know when you are ready when you are so o.k. with yourself that you don't need ANYTHING to feel complete.

THAT'S when the Universe will shower you with all the gifts of life.

I know it sounds ironic. You get everything when you need nothing. You see the same dynamic energy in relationships. If someone is overly eager to be with you, it pushes you away. But if they don't want you or play hard to get, then suddenly you are attracted to them. It's the same with money and everything else. If you are needy or desperate, you are pushing it away. But if you become self-sufficient, suddenly money comes from everywhere.

So the secret my friends is NOT to go after the money, you will push it away. Make yourself self-sufficient, have the courage to follow your heart, be yourself and life will take care of you.

Start by finding peace in your life and doing what makes you feel good. THIS IS ABSOLUTELY NECESSARY.

Just make sure you've upgraded your inner programming.

Remember- Prosperous people create the life they want. Poor people think life just happens to them. Are you on the creating or the receiving end?

Oh yeah. As you know I am a romantic. I used to always say "Money doesn't matter, only love matters." And guess what? I had romance but no money. Stop going around being self-righteous and saying love is all that matters and money doesn't. OK, well in a way, it's true, we both have good intentions when saying that, but we need to realize we are comparing apples and oranges. Of course love matters. But money is important too. These two subjects should never be in the same sentence. This is like comparing car repairs with a frog. Huh?

People say we should be in a barter system. Sure that's great for small local stuff, but if you call the airlines and say "Yes, I'd like a roundtrip flight to Austria, I have two goats and a chicken for payment..." I can guarantee you will will hear something sounding like a click followed by a dial tone.

Let's say you want to buy a new car. I don't think Ford or BMW will go for the goat and chicken either. Neither will the electric company, the water company, the gas station or any of the other big living expenses in your life that require lots of real money to operate. And those are your biggest expenses. Bottom line is- YOU NEED MONEY.

So get over the poverty hippie-thinking right now. Money is just as important as love. If anyone comes to you in the future and gives you that old love and money line, look them in the eye and remind them how broke they are, and you are tired of their bitching and to go out there and get a life WITH love AND money and feel good about it. Money does not corrupt, all it does is amplify who you already are.

There is a line in a song "Love won't pay my bills" and it's true.

Watch what you say

Positive energy attracts. Negative energy pushes away. Be constantly aware of what you say and how you say it, especially sarcasm. Your subconscious doesn't know the difference between dark humor and dark reality. Joke about something and attract it. Most of what we say leans either towards the positive side or the negative side. Make a conscious effort to always keep it on the "up" side. It may be hard at first because sarcasm is very tempting to use nowadays. People automatically use it to bond with a stranger. It's used as an opening line between men. Men use sarcasm a lot because they are afraid of intimacy, they see it as a vulnerability. Do you want to wallow with the lower class mentality? I suggest you become a role model to others and show some class. You will be amazed how quickly the Universe starts responding to the new you with classier things in your life.

From this moment on, become aware of the energy behind everything you think and say- for example- some people may think "I don't want to be poor anymore" is a constructive declaration, but it's not. It's actually negative. If someone told you "Don't think about your dog" What happens?" You think about your dog- you can't help it. If someone says "I don't want to think about bills", guess what- they think about bills. The brain thinks about <u>anything</u> that's mentioned, no matter what context the sentence is in. It's very curious, like a jealous immature paranoid child. So by saying "I don't want to be poor anymore.", your brain focusses on "DON'T" (a negative word) and "POOR", (a very negative word). Whatever you think about, you attract, so by thinking this way, you are actually attracting poorness. By saying "I hope my spouse never cheats" is putting fearful negative energy into the air, and actually starts attracting the very thing you are afraid of. It is the way of nature. When you run from an animal, it runs after you and eats you. But if you casually stick around and go "Hey, how's it going?", it sits there staring at you, but doesn't attack. In life, you need to learn to not focus on the bad or you will attract it.

So from now on, do NOT say *"I don't want to be poor anymore"*, say *"You know what? I'm doing the rich thing now. I'm just gonna go for it, no matter what."*

Focus on the answer, not the problem. The dream, not the nightmare. The whole, not the hole.

Don't focus your energy on the problem, focus on the benefits of the new life. Don't give one more thought or moment of your life to anything negative. Start introducing yourself to the good stuff in life. There are no problems, only opportunities.

Always remember, what you say, do and think attracts either success or stuff you don't want. The choice is yours.

Stop Wanting

Once you know what you want, stop wanting it and just get it.

"Wanting" something means just that- wanting. In other words, you don't have it, you just want it. You can "want" something your whole life and never get it. You need to take action and actually get it. As silly as this sounds, it's true and a big reason people don't get anything- they just sit around wishing and imagining from a distance, while something inside them feels it's probably an unrealistic goal. Kind of like an overweight bald guy dreaming of a beautiful girl. He just sits there all his life looking at pictures, and never once even tries to approach one because he feels he doesn't have a chance in hell. He's already pre-judged himself and determined his future. I can't tell you how many times I have seen a super hot girl with some guy that looks like a hairy penguin. She can have any guy she wants and she picks THIS gnome? Of course people will say she's obviously in it for the money. Perhaps. But things are not always as they seem. Maybe she's had it with the slick, good looking fast-talking players and wants someone real she feels comfortable with. You never know. The point is, that first guy who spends his life "wanting" but not doing anything about it has doomed himself to never living his dream. Stop assuming. You can do anything if you believe it. Anything.

So what have we learned here? Not to use the word "want". The same goes for the word "try", because it means "attempt" which is not the same as actually successfully doing something. Remember when Luke Skywalker said "*I'll try...*", Yoda replied "*That is why you fail.*"

Sure you'll fail lots of times. The rich don't care. They know pain and failures are gifts to learn from. They are wakeup calls.

"Would you like me to give you a formula for success? It's quite simple, really. Double your rate of failure. You are thinking of failure as the enemy of success. But it isn't at all. You can be discouraged by failure or you can learn from it, So go ahead and make mistakes. Make all you can. Because that's where you will find success."

Thomas J. Watson

Take a good look in the mirror, What do you see? What do you feel? Do you see a millionaire in the mirror? Do you feel like a Millionaire? Because if you don't you won't be one. You need to already "be there" in your spirit. You need to be vibrating with it, tasting it with every cell of your being. It's like when you met the love of your life and you knew right then and there THAT was the person you would end up with- you just knew it! I was the same way with my homes. As the real estate agent was driving me up the road, as the house came into view, I knew right away THAT was going to be the house- before I even went inside, I just knew it. The same with my cars, my friends... everything. I can feel it. It's like I can look into the future and see myself there with that person, place or thing. There is no doubt, no question, no fear, just a feeling of completeness and perfection. That's what you need to feel about your future as a success in whatever it is. You can't "want" it, you have to already see , taste and feel it. <u>The future is as real as this moment</u>. Past, present and future are one. You ARE there now. No more waiting, you have become the Millionaire. You feel at peace and excited at the same time.

"We don't see things as they are. We see things as we are." Anais Nin

You can't kid yourself into being like this. You can't kid the Universe. This has to be genuinely real. If it isn't, you still have some work to do. Something inside still doesn't believe you deserve it. You need to feel like you are just as good as any of those rich people. You need to be one of them. You need to picture yourself hanging out at the country club with your rich friends.

Country club ?? What did you just feel when I said that?

Did you think *"Ewww, that's not me. Those people are stodgy boring old farts. I am definitely not one of those! No way."*

Or did you think *"I don't know, they'll probably see right through me and see me for the small time wannabe that I am."*

Or *"I will never fit in with the rich crowd. They're so fake. I want to just be the down-to-earth T-shirt guy hanging loose with my friends."*

If you had any kind of thought where you felt like you didn't fit in with the rich crowd for some reason, then you exposed one of your self-worth parasites that stop you from ever becoming rich. It was probably put there a long time ago and strengthened every time you hung out with your poverty-minded friends who constantly talk down about rich people. You need to wipe this clean. You MUST see yourself as deserving to be rich- equal with other people on top. You need to seriously boost your self-worth. Have you been cut down and made to feel small and worthless by someone or people at any point in your life? Why do you see rich people as any better than you?

Rich people aren't any better, smarter or different. They are just rich, that's all. And they have no problem with that. You obviously do, otherwise you would be up there with them.

Success in almost any field depends more on energy and drive than it does on intelligence. This explains why we have so many stupid leaders. Sloan Wilson

Watch who you hang out with

This is a fascinating subject. As you know by now, everything is energy and energy is contagious. Being around positive upbeat people makes you feel good. Being around depressing people makes you depressed. The same goes for money energy. It has been said that your income is the average of your five closest friends. In other words- take the five people you hang around the most with, add up their incomes and divide by five- that is probably what you are making. It's pretty amazing.

Your life has been affected and shaped by the energy, thoughts and expectations of those around you whether you want it or not. Who you hang out with (share energy with) influences your income and level of success. Their values become yours.

If you want to become prosperous and happy, then hang around prosperous and happy people. I hate to say it, but you may have to distance yourself from your downer friends who have no money and talk down about others. I'm sure they're wonderful nice people overall, but these kind of people are keeping you down. Be nice to them, but get on with your life. This is not a cruel insensitive thing to do, because the only thing that will really motivate people to change, is being inspired by others, especially someone they know. You need to show them that's it's possible for someone to break free from poverty and "make it". You need to be their hero, and the only way you can do that is prove to them it works by being a living example.

Never shrink down to other people's level. Inspire them to rise to yours. Speaking of inspiration- rich people don't resent other rich people- they are inspired by them, look at them as role models and learn from them.

Poor people on the other hand are bitter, competitive and judgmental when someone is more successful. They sneer and talk bad about them behind their back, not knowing the Universe is standing right there listening. The investor just got turned off.

For one man who can stand prosperity, there are a hundred that will stand adversity. Elvis Presley

Negativity is Poison

I will say this again and again. Negativity is a disease of the human brain. Most animals don't have it. It is a terrible virus. Negativity is not the same as sensibility. Some people say it's "being realistic". The irony is that yes, it becomes their reality. Whatever negative thoughts they have actually start manifesting in their lives because they are attracting it. Whatever you put thought or energy into becomes real. So be careful! Your mind is one of the most powerful forces on the planet and most people have no clue how to control it. It's like being in a room of scared people randomly shooting guns in all directions.

It's simple- positive energy creates, negative energy destroys.

If you resent the rich, you will remain poor. It's that simple.

If someone is better off than you, congratulate them (without any expectations for handouts in return!)

Do NOT resent others for being smarter, better looking, richer, more successful, famous, or having nicer things. As a matter of fact, you should cheer them on, because remember- it all comes back to you!

How do you stop yourself from resenting others and actually be happy for them? The best way to wish them well is to find some kind of relief in your own life ...something to feel good about. The other day I was on a long road trip with no where to pull over to take a wizz. My bladder felt like it was going to burst and I wasn't too happy about other cars on the road. Finally I pulled over when I got a chance and woooow, what an amazing feeling of relief. I was in heaven. No money in the world can give me that kind of relief. I felt like I was floating on a cloud. I got back in my car and felt so high on life, that I was happy for every car on the road, I wished them all well, I felt we were all connected as one. I was celebrating life WITH them and actually singing. It's amazing how loving and positive we are when we find relief in our own world. Our entire perspective changes. Other people didn't change, but our view of them did. The way to feel good about rich people is to start feeling good about yourself. And one the best ways is to get rid of whatever's burdening you.

You need to Relieve Yourself!

Stay away from negative people and situations as much as possible. They will poison you and drain your resources. This includes family and friends. They may be well meaning, loving people, but if they are infected with the negativity bug, keep your distance, including what you say to them. For example, when I used to get close to something good and profitable happening, I would be so excited, I told my parents and friends about it, including some down-and-out people I knew, telling them I would help them financially when the money came through. The reaction was the same from all of them- almost no reaction at all... because none of them believed it would really happen. It was the same "I'll believe it when I see it" and "I've heard that one a million times before... what makes you think it's going to happen <u>this</u> time??" We've all had this. You can just feel their negativity pulling the fun and excitement out of the air. You can hear the music dying in your head. And guess what happens... nothing. No money, no deal. And they all shrug their shoulders with the "I thought so" and "I told you so". I learned to stop doing that. And everything changed.

By the way- be careful even AFTER the money comes through, they will have the "easy come, easy go" opinion, and sure enough the money will be taken away as fast as it came to you.

BE CAREFUL !!! Don't tell people when you have potential money coming in (or anything prosperous). Bitter or negative people can blow it for you energetically. When you get a gift from the Universe, thank the universe, but don't brag about it to others, no matter how good your intentions are. If you want to share and give your friends some of it, fine, but don't tell them how you got it. Keep it a mystery, because I guarantee you, their energy will sabotage any further success if you let them, because they are <u>disbelievers</u>. This is poison to success. Guard your treasure. The universe (your investor) is testing and trusting you.

Negative people tend to hang out together because they like to bitch a lot and feel sorry for themselves. Rich people like to hang out with successful, prosperous, high-frequency people and situations. They get energy and more motivation from it. They are like solar panels collecting LIGHT, because positive energy is light, and negative energy is darkness. Prosperous people give off a powerful aura- you can spot them easily in a room, they exude an energy poor people never have. They are confident, powerful, relaxed and have serious presence. People are naturally attracted to them. It's all energy my friends and you can't fake it. It comes from within.

Sure there are some bad ones, but most aren't. You just hear about the odd bad one more because they are more powerful and affect more people than the average person. Plus, it makes great news. Poor people love to see a successful person crumble, it makes them feel good, they are like vultures. It also makes better news because, well, nobody cares if some small-time unknown poor person does something bad- that's to be expected anyway, right?

Another trait of poor people is they despise any form of self-promotion, advertising, or someone selling something. They say *"He's just doing it for the money"* Oh come on.

Rich people promote. Poor people de-mote.

If we could harness all the energy that poor people spend every day cutting others down, we would solve the world's energy problem!

Rich people look for solutions. Poor people look for problems. There will always be challenges, no matter who you are. The difference is how you handle it. Rich people look at a problem and go "Hmmm". Poor people just complain and whine.

Success is how high you bounce when you hit bottom.
George S. Patton

Stop competing

Poor people compete. It's their ego controlling them. Rich people respect each other. For example, you may notice when driving on the freeway, poor and middle class people race. They want to pass you. If you speed up, they speed up. They do not want you to be faster than them. It is so easy to activate somebody's ego on the highway. It's amazing how hair-trigger the competition mindset is among most people. They cut you off, act like idiots and drive like maniacs, just to prove they are superior. This totally reflects their view and position in life.

The other day, I was zooming down a freeway in the Mohave desert when I ended up next to a Rolls Royce also doing 100 like me. It was going fast but not weaving through traffic like others. There was a slow car up ahead. Some little car with a loud muffler zoomed in from out of nowhere and swerved through us like some annoying little gnat and roared off. The Rolls elegantly put its turn signal on to change lanes and waited for me to pass, but I flashed my lights to let him in. He responded by tapping his taillights twice to let me know he was thankful. There is such a class distinction it's difficult for words to describe. We didn't have to compete. We didn't feel threatened. We had nothing to prove. We were comfortable with our lives, and as a result, our two energies combined as one, making us stronger than if we were two separate competing egos. How are you driving the highway of life?

This is the difference between rich and poor.

The Direction of Energy

There is no way to prosperity, prosperity is the way. Wayne Dyer

Energy flows and creates life, but in which direction is it flowing? Most people are good at sending OUT energy. They are loud and restless and can't stop spending money. Poor people make a lot of noise, they pound their chest, they have big giant pickup trucks and muscle cars with loud mufflers. They love to give you their piece of mind and they love shooting their guns and their finger. This is all energy going OUT.

Rich people listen. They study and they learn. They don't go after things, they let things come to them. Money comes to them because the energy flows IN towards them. They are receivers.

An interesting phenomenon I've noticed is poor people don't like hand-outs. I'm not talking about street beggars, I'm talking about a normal family living in a home, struggling to make ends meet. When you try to offer them a bit of money, they won't take it. They say "Oh no, we couldn't!" They are not comfortable with receiving.

If you offered the same little donation to the rich person, as silly as it seems, I guarantee you they will take it with a chuckle and smile.

You see- that little donation is a message from the Universe- it's testing you. Why would it give you a lot, when you have trouble receiving even a little? You are constantly being tested. Sometimes it puts a coin on the sidewalk. That is your test. Do not look at it as simply a penny. Look at it as MONEY. It's all just a symbol. Paper money is just paper. The copper in that penny is actual worth more than the paper used to make a 100 dollar bill. If you see a penny or any coin- IT IS MONEY. Accept it. Make it yours. Hold it up and say "Thank you Universe for this sign. I appreciate everything!"

You need to be able to graciously be able to receive. First you will be tested with small stuff to see if you are even able to receive. When you open a Paypal account, it does the same thing... they send you 3 cents to test and make sure your bank account is ready to receive before allowing the big money to flow.

Think about it. You go out of your way to offer someone a gift, and they refuse it. What an insult! Remember what I said earlier- you need to be able to APPRECIATE, and receiving is a form of appreciation. The Universe is not going to give anything to someone who doesn't appreciate or receive openly. Stop being a martyr and start accepting!!!! You will make the giver happier by accepting, rather than by graciously refusing. People (and the Universe) LOVE to give. So start receiving. As a matter of fact, open a bank account to prepare.

"If you build it, he will come"

Clear the clutter from your house and life so you are ready to receive new exciting things.

Create a vacuum so things start coming to you to fill the hole. Have you ever noticed how painful it is to end a relationship?

Why? Because we are afraid- *"What if I don't find anything better?" "What if I'm alone for the rest of my life?", "Who will take care of me?"* etc. Yet what happens the moment we create a hole? It's filled with something (or someone) new. This is the way energy works. Look at your garage or any other storage space.

The same with money and everything else. Clear the way. Prepare. Make ready.

Remember, part of the clearing process is getting rid of your old negative fearful thought patterns that have been blocking the prosperity energy from flowing into your life.

If it's not flowing, there is a blockage somewhere.

You need a life enema!

Success consists of going from failure to failure without loss of enthusiasm.
Winston Churchill

By the way, speaking of enemas (my favorite subject), since everything is connected more than you know, to help get things going, I suggest you read my book "Heal Yourself 101" and do the body cleanse. You will be amazed how clear your head becomes, making it easier to make decisions and be in a healthier, more relaxed state of mind. The modern lifestyle is very toxic... stress, bread, sugar, processed carbs, cooked food, trans fats and pretty much anything most people eat clogs up the liver, kidneys, and creates brain plaque, making it hard for your brain to function. You will be amazed how a lot of your negativity washes away when you do a thorough body cleanse. It has been scientifically proven that an oxygen-starved brain becomes very irritable, cranky, sour and negative. People with a clogged liver have anger issues. This has been known for thousands of years. People with toxic kidneys are emotional basket cases and cry a lot. This is discussed in my book "Heal Your Face". It's all connected! It's very possible that by simply cleaning your body and only putting healthy natural living food back in, that you will feel so much better that your new positive energy brings in new ideas and inspiration that can actually get you out of the financial rut you're in. I get emails regularly from people saying it changed their entire life. It made them new people and helped propel them into a new way of thinking. This is the basis of prosperity and success!

Stress is a big part of health problems, and money problems cause stress. It goes both ways. If you get one part of your life under control, it makes it easier for the other parts. So hit it from all sides. When you get your health under control and you start to look younger again, you start getting confidence again, which gives you peace and inspiration to now tackle your finances. When you feel good, you can do anything.

Real Currency

Another interesting note about energy direction is rich people tend to buy things that go up in value over time, whereas poor people buy things that go down in value.

One interesting message in my "Free Food and Medicine" DVD sets is that the REAL currency on this planet is not money, it's seeds, because seeds grow into plants that give us food, medicine, clothing, lumber, power and life. Seeds grow plants which grow more plants which have more seeds which grow endless more plants that can ultimately feed, clothe, heal and power the entire planet. Without seeds, we would be dead. Animals would have nothing to eat. There would be no life.

What kind of food do most poor people eat? Junk food. ... processed, cooked dead mush that comes from a box, jar, bag, bottle or can. If you plant it in the ground, nothing grows but mold because it's not really food anymore, just empty calories that give you a quick burst of energy but rot your body, in other words- poor people eat food that gives them instant gratification.

If you've ever been to a really high class restaurant, you'll notice the food is not deep-fried or squished out of a machine. It actually still looks like it did in nature for the most part. Have you ever wondered why the portions are smaller at expensive upper class places? I mean, they're charging enough right? The longest living people eat very little. They don't pig out on heavy carbs. They don't eat an entire bag of potato chips before guzzling half a gallon of beer, then eat twenty pancakes with heavy sugary syrup with a side of bacon and sausage and finishing off with a candy bar and ice cream between meals.

When you live at a higher vibration, you don't eat that way anymore. Sure a good number of rich people do, but they don't last long. The point is, the more you model your life around natural design, the more able you are to prosper. Poor people love to eat junk- instant gratification. Rich people treat money like seeds- the true currency of the planet. They buy things that can multiply in value, like seeds.

What about the hippies that eat healthy? You know- the spiritual seekers who want to live in harmony with nature and keep their footprint on the Earth to a minimum. They eat super healthy, so why aren't they rich?

Because they don't want to be. They're very uncomfortable with the thought. Many of them came from the upbringing of the 60's where the "system" was bad. Anything that had to do with big business (the "suits"), money, government was corrupt. The government was sending innocent people to war to kill more innocent people elsewhere, and why? For oil and money. To hippies, oil pollutes and money corrupts. The world was becoming very complicated, confusing and overwhelming, so the natural reaction is to run away and get back to basics and nature.

Nothing wrong with that.

Except for the mental programming that money and material things are bad. They think barter is the only way. Like I said earlier, you can't buy a car or pay utility companies with goats and chickens. Many people in the "new age" world have money issues and although they might outwardly say peace and love are all that mater, it won't pay the bills. So they are frustrated and inwardly resentful of successful people. This is negative energy and goes against what they preach. Rich people are not meaner or worse than poor people. They just have more money, freedom and power. Everybody wants to save the world, but it's very difficult to help others when you are broke and bumming off of others. Anyone who blames others for their problems is in victim-mode and poverty consciousness. Yes there are mean selfish people, but we live in this world anyway despite them.

The Universe cannot exist without balance. Extremists don't last. There must be balance.

You can't just sit there and meditate- you have to actually DO something. Go out there and get a life. The clock is ticking.

So to sum up this chapter- you must start seeing every penny, every dollar as a SEED that can produce more seeds. Do not eat all your seeds because they taste good, keep a few so you can replant them. This is a big difference between rich and poor.

Self-sufficiency is key in the world of food, money, health ... everything. It is the one thing (other than Love) that I promote more than anything. Self-sufficiency is paramount. It is sustainability. It brings peace, confidence and a base upon which to build your empire of prosperity.

Energy direction is so important. You can use your personal energy level as a gauge. Do the people around you support you and make you feel energized, or do they drain you and make you feel tired?

Does what you do for a living energize or drain you?

Does your house nurture and heal you or is it one big drain?

Is your car a financial drain?

Do you feel like you are just running around plugging leaks ?

List all the things that you run around doing all day that take your time, energy and money and figure out how you can get rid of them.

You need energy coming to you, not being drained out.

Break the Comfort Zone

Most people won't change unless they have to or are in an emergency situation, meaning most people won't change. The comfort zone is a prison. Life begins where the comfort zone ends. You grow by breaking through your old skin and stepping outside your comfort zone. This is another big difference. Poor people like to stay in their comfort zone. They don't want to risk much. They like having the warm familiar stuff to come home to at night. Nothing wrong with that if that's where they want to be the rest of their life, with the same problems, worries and money issues. Comfort and convenience are what keeps people numb and poor. This doesn't mean the rich aren't comfortable. But they took a chance and made a wild dash through the freezing cold from their warm sleeping bag in the campground, ... to the nice luxury hotel a mile down the road.

If what you are doing now is not getting you the results you want, then you have to try something different, probably something new you've never done before. This is scary. You have to step outside the boundaries you are comfortable with. This is new territory. It is the only way to grow. You must try new things. You may fail a few times before you get it right, but unless you put your feet forward and start walking, you are going nowhere. Stumbling is part of learning to walk. Walking is part of learning to run. Stop waiting for something to magically fall into your lap. Open the door, get out there and meet new people. Get off your ass and don't be afraid to fail. It's part of learning and growing. As strange as it sounds, rich people don't like to be comfortable for very long. They have this constant itch to try new things and step into new uncomfortable territory.

The ultimate measure of a man is not where he stands in moments of comfort and convenience, but where he stands at times of challenge and controversy.

Martin Luther King Jr.

It's simple- do you want to spend your life wondering what could have been? ...or do you want to find out?!

One way is merely existing, the other is truly living.

Sometimes you win, sometimes you lose. But if you stay at it long enough, the winning starts exceeding the losing. There is a pattern among rich people. They make it, they lose everything... they make it, they lose it, they make it, they lose it ... they make it, they make it, they make it. They learn from their mistakes and start dialing in a winning formula that works for them. You would never get that just sitting around waiting.

Discouragement and failure are two of the surest stepping stones to success.

Dale Carnegie

Clear the Way for Success

If there is one simple way to sum up this book it would be this. Always remember, the truth is really simple. It requires no thought, just acceptance. If something seems too complicated or overwhelming, get out of there, it is something lacking identity and will do nothing but drain precious time from your life.

The secret to ANY kind of success, prosperity, freedom or accomplishment ...is to clear anything in the way of that.

It's that simple.

Clear the way for success.

What's usually in the way?

- your thoughts.
- other people's thoughts and opinions.
- your fears
- other people's fears
- the past
- preconceived notions of how something is, or going to be
- judgement
- lack of motivation (a form of fear and life clutter)
- a cluttered house
- a cluttered relationship
- cluttered finances
- owning too many things
- too many responsibilities

- too many bills
- a cluttered gummed up body
- negativity from friends, family, media
- pessimism
- bad experiences in the past
- resentment, jealousy
- comparing yourself to others

The list goes on as long as you let it.

The more you clear these things out of the way, the more of a path you clear. Success already exists. It doesn't have to be created. All you have to do is let it in. Open the door and have a clean empty space for it to fill. Simply ALLOW it into your life. Become a nice person and lay out the welcome mat. Treat success like it's a super wealthy person coming to visit you, and can read your mind. If you were success, would you like to be living with you? Or are you too much of a downer? Someone who keeps cutting themselves down? Would you want to work with you? Would you invest in you? Or are there too many loose ends and distractions. Success wants someone who has no distractions- someone who can totally focus and is obsessed with achieving. Someone full of life that fires up everyone they meet.

All people really want is to feel good. They want feel good energy. Do you have that? That's what success wants to hang out with. Don't depress success.

Keep Learning and Growing

Energy keeps moving, changing and flowing. It's never the same. Successful people know this and flow with life. They are constantly updating, learning and adapting with the times. They study people richer than them. Adapt or die, it's a cardinal rule of nature. Poor people think they know it all. Rich people keep learning new stuff. If poor people are so smart, why aren't they rich? Most of the endless babble that poor people try to impress you with is nothing more than justification. Rich people don't need to justify anything.

Poor people "don't have the time"

Rich people make time.

Keep up with the times or else you are history.

Notice the word "learn" contains the word "earn".

Those who know, grow.

I know a lot of you will say you know this stuff already. Of course you do. We all know this deep inside. So I ask you... why aren't you rich? The answer is you either don't believe it, have missed a key element, or keep putting it off to another day because your daily emergencies are just too important, ...or you simply made an inner choice that you are comfortable where you are and have made an unconscious decision to not change, and that's fine.

MEET THE RICH

Ok, you've been to school, now it's time for the field trip. One of the best ways to start convincing yourself that what you've just read is true, and begin changing the way you think about prosperity and wealth, is to actually meet some of the rich and prosperous people on top... the ones who have made it. I am now going to introduce you to three of my powerful friends. They all started from nothing and are now super prosperous. They are friends with the biggest, most famous people on Earth. I told them to share their secrets with you. I picked these three because they are all completely unique with very different backgrounds, but you will start to see the same common traits in each one. Keep in mind as you read these, that YOU can be right there with them, and if you feel you are not in their league or can't be prosperous like them and free to do what you want, or that it's not righteous to be successful, then you need to re-read this book !

So without further delay, may I introduce you to the world of the super successful. I will see you again at the end of the book to say some final words.

Marshall Sylver

When Marshall walked through my door for the first time years ago, he exuded power. He is one of the most confident people I have ever met and it was obvious he knew what he was doing in life. Yet he's a real person and when I spoke, I had his full attention. He was not "too busy" like all the other people I knew who were running around in a panic with too many responsibilities. Marshall is real. He literally lives in a palace here in Las Vegas, and also has the biggest house on the beach in San Diego. I know, because I've been to both. He rented Richard Branson's island just to have a family get-together. How many people can say that? Yes he has a Rolls Royce. He's quite well known for helping the less fortunate. He is real. You want success, here it is. The following are two chapters from books Marshall has written and allowed me to share with you.

Whether on stage or in the corporate boardroom, Marshall Sylver helps people realize their deepest dreams. His dramatic stage and television shows have earned him the title, "The Greatest Hypnotist of All Time." Yet he's increasingly sought after as a business consultant to Fortune 500 clients because of a personal development program he created titled "Subconscious Reprogramming." Marshall teaches individuals how to develop successful business disciplines by mastering their internal "drivers" that create their habits. "Most people are responding to suggestions all the time about who they are, or aren't, and what they can, or cannot do." From the time he was a young child and used hypnosis to cure himself of insomnia, Marshall has believed that hypnosis can be used to improve the quality of life and communication. Watch Marshall use his mastery of hypnosis and learn more about his dynamic seminars at www.sylver.com.

Part I – Think Rich

How to Unleash Your "Inner" Prosperity

Develop a Millionaire Mindset
By Marshall Sylver

****

"Do you think that it is possible for you to be a millionaire? That there are a million ways to be a millionaire? My guess is that you do. So if that's possible, then the only reason you aren't a millionaire is – you!

I want to help you change from the inside out, so you can think about creating wealth the way a millionaire does. When you do, you'll make massive amounts of money – in fact, you won't be able to stop the flow of money into your life!

Rich people think differently than poor people. I'm not talking about rich people who earn a million dollars or more a year by working 70 and 80 hours a week, sacrificing their family, their health, and their wellbeing in the process, all in pursuit of the Almighty Dollar. I'm talking about earning money joyfully. Wouldn't that be wonderful, living a life that joyfully creates wealth?

The right financial habits can help you do that. In my seminars, I teach a technique I developed called "Psycho Neuro Duplication." Simply understood, by thinking what someone successful thinks, and then doing what they do, you become successful, too. It's a simple process, but one that demands discipline. When you think what a slender, fit person thinks and then do what they do, you'll become slender and fit, too.

There's no secret "skinny" gene.   It's the same with the financial habits that can make you wealthy.

By my definition, anyone who isn't earning a million dollars a year joyfully is a pauper. If hearing that makes you uneasy, or even angry, I'm glad. That reaction may push you to change your beliefs and actions so you finally can stop struggling with money. I can almost hear you saying, "That's easy for you to say, Marshall, as you drive in your Rolls Royce and fly in a private jet. You don't know what it's like to be kicked out of your apartment for not being able to pay the rent."

Actually, I do know what it's like, which is why I'm the perfect person to teach you about wealth. I was born and raised on a farm in Michigan with no running water, no electricity, and often, little, and sometimes no, food. After my first home was condemned, my second home was a converted chicken coop. Other than making me very grateful for my humble roots, the only other side effect is that I tend to cluck when I get nervous (only kidding!).

My humble beginnings helped me see things differently. At seven years old, I saw quite clearly that we were the poorest family in my community. Everyone else had more than my family, and many families made a lot of money. I knew they weren't smarter than me, or more creative, harder working, or better looking. I saw that they did things differently. They held different beliefs about life, and they took different actions. The biggest difference? They focused on making money, not holding onto it so tightly out of fear of the unknown.

If all of the money in the world was divided evenly among all of the people, within five years, it would be right back in the same hands again. Why? People who know how to make money would keep making money, and hardworking, positive, motivated, intelligent people would stay poor, and for the same reason – because of their habits.

Let's start talking about how you can change the habits that keep you poor, and instead adopt the "millionaire mindset" that will transform your life and make you wealthy. The novelist F. Scott Fitzgerald said, "The rich are different than you and I." In my book of life, there are three big differences.

Distinction #1:
Millionaires eliminate minimum wage activities from their lives.

As long as you fill up your day with minimum wage activities, it's not possible to be a millionaire. Do you take out your own trash? Pick up around the house? Do your own laundry? If you answered "Yes!" to any of those questions, then you're involved in minimum wage activities. If you want to generate a million dollars, or more, in revenue every year, then you must recognize that money is math. To do that, joyfully or otherwise, based on a 40-hour work week, 50 weeks a year, your time is worth $500 an hour minimum. Any action someone else can do for less doesn't fit millionaire habits.

See which minimum wage activities you can eliminate from your life. Start looking at more efficient ways to live your life, and take action.

For example, do you spend two hours arguing about a cell phone bill because the phone company overcharged you $10?

If you are, you'll never be a millionaire, because, even if you win, you only made $5 an hour from that discussion. You may say, "Well, it's the principle." The principle is, You are struggling and you don't deserve to struggle. Would a millionaire spend two hours a night watching cable television? Probably not –unless they owned the network! A millionaire consistently asks themselves, "What is the highest and best use of my time?"

Abraham Lincoln said that if you have one hour to chop down a tree, spend 40 minutes sharpening the axe. You could chop down the tree by slamming it with a dull axe. The tree may fall after an hour, but your hands will be bruised and blistered and you won't be able to chop down the next tree. If, however, you spend 40 minutes sharpening that ax, in the next 20 minutes, you can chop down the tree with little effort. In fact, because you sharpened the axe and did the foundational work in the beginning, you then can chop down the next tree, and the next, and the next.

Letting go of instantaneous gratification is the lesson here, and in the long run it creates wealth. If you work 40, 50, and even 60 hours per week, and come home at night exhausted, you can't afford cable TV. I'm not talking about the monthly fee; you can't afford spending those two hours when you could spend them sharpening your "ax."

You may be uncomfortable at first, but remember the principle: Money is math. You have the same hours in your day as a millionaire or billionaire who knows how to best utilize their time and resources. As you do, you'll begin to grow to a place where you no longer have to trade hours for dollars.

The media has dubbed me "The Greatest Hypnotist of All Time," but what I do isn't magic; it's mindset.

Like me, you were probably raised by parents who wanted you to have a better life, but they may not have motivated you in ways that were successful. When I was growing up, my mother would tell me, "Marshall, work hard, get ahead," and she meant well, but her mindset hindered my life for years. This angel on earth raised 10 children, largely on her own, and worked three jobs to put food on the table for us, but her idea of creating greater wealth was to sleep one less hour so that she could work one more hour.

For years, I traded my precious hours for too few dollars. I was always asking myself, "How can I get more work done?", and always struggling, until one day in my early 20s. I was searching frantically for enough spare change in the couch to buy a package of Kraft Macaroni 'n Cheese. I managed the apartment complex where I was living, but was about to be kicked out because I couldn't afford even the discounted rent. I realized I had to start clearing my mind of the pauper thoughts that were holding me captive. I started asking, "How can I create more wealth?", and as I did, I began to see a second big difference between millionaires and paupers:

Distinction #2:
Millionaires upgrade the value of their time.

What do you think is more valuable, a Moped or a Rolls Royce? A Rolls Royce, of course – unless you live on a mountain, with goat paths for roads. Depending on where you live, a Moped is far more valuable. What I'm saying is, What something costs has nothing to do with its value; it's what others are willing to pay that matters.

You are rewarded in life by what you create as value for someone else. Look at all the new service businesses and products we have today that didn't exist 20, 10 or even five years ago. Could you ever imagine that someday, you might pay a "pet-sitter," while you were at work or on vacation? Did you ever think you would spend $5 for a cup of coffee, $1 for a bottle of water, or use a "sponge-less" mop to clean up a spill? How many times have you seen a product advertised on television or in a store and thought, "I wish I had come up with that idea. What a timesaver!"? You can create value for others with the most common, or most exotic, idea or concept.

To create wealth, you also have to upgrade the value of your time, so that others are willing to pay for it. How do you do that? Give more than you ask. Remember that those who receive the value of what you create determine its value. If you had paid every dollar you have to buy this book – if you paid a million dollars – it's worth it, if my words inspired you to go out and make billions.

Distinction #3:
Millionaires ask, How much will I make from this opportunity?

As a millionaire, I know that I have to take risks to create wealth; I must put my money, my reputation, and my talents on the line. Millionaires constantly look at the upside and seldom focus on the downside. If something costs me $1 million to buy, but earns $1.5 million, cost is irrelevant.

Paupers are always concerned with cost, because they have a very limited view of what is possible. How much faith and follow through are you willing to give to launching your own business?

Faith = follow through

To be an entrepreneur means you will be moving ahead without clear direction, and often in the face of fear. When everyone else gives up, you have the energy and enough belief in yourself to keep going. You understand your customers, because you work hard at understanding what they want. You're confident about your goal, so that others will follow you because they want to share the faith and adventure you instill in them. For you to be able to lead and persuade others towards your vision, you must possess these three specific skills:

Skill# 1:
Control Your Thoughts and Emotions

You may already have a good idea of how wealthy people – athletes, entertainers, and real estate tycoons – make millions of dollars joyfully every year, so there are only two reasons why you don't have what you want right now. Either you don't know the ABCs of making your dreams come true, or, if you do, you can't get off the couch to take consistent action on a regular basis.

Want to lose weight? After years of study, scientific research, thousands of examples and cases of people who were successful at taking the fat off of their body that they wanted to take off, we have come up with a genuine formula that works every single time: Eat Less – Move More!

Want to make more money naturally? Apply the same thinking: Work Less – Add More Value!

What if how you lived your life on a daily basis brought great joy to you? What if what you thought created wealth and attracted financial security to you? In this chapter, start thinking like a millionaire – even if the money hasn't been deposited into your bank account yet.

<u>Skill #2:</u> Use the Right Tools

Most companies are started by people who figured out how to "build a better mousetrap." Leverage a great idea, or create your own – it doesn't matter. Figure out how to do a business better; that's the path to wealth.

Learning to sell and market your idea is critical, and knowing effective business systems is so important, that I devote much of the next chapter to describing this one external set of tools. By having the right tools, you understand the processes that others have used to create wealth, and you use them for yourself.

<u>Skill #3:</u> Take Action in the Present Moment

When? Right now. "Tomorrow" never comes. What you don't do in this moment, most likely you'll never do at all. If you're like most people – if you don't exercise in the morning –, chances are you won't, as the day's demands and distractions mount up. That's unfortunate, because what keeps you healthy and on track should be the highest priority of your day, not the lowest. Do yourself a favor and circle the word "Action" above.

No risk, no reward. Millionaires know that at times, they have to "fail forward fast" to become wealthy. They know that not all seeds fall on fertile soil; that's just a part of the game.

If you've ever played the game Monopoly, you know there's a very specific strategy to winning: You buy every single property you land on. Do that, and halfway through the game, you'll run out of money. It looks like other people, who have more money than you, are winning. To buy more property, you now have to borrow against your existing properties, often reaping half their value and paying lots of interest. When everyone runs out of property, though, you're be able to cash in, because those properties are now income-generating assets. By playing on that strategy, you'll always win.

Such thoughts are common to a millionaire's mindset. You'll begin to notice that paupers jump on the stock market, real estate or business bandwagon, when rich people are jumping off with their profits. Buy low, sell high. Buy when everyone is selling. Leverage other people's creativity. To become a shepherd, do the exact opposite of what the sheep are doing.

Remembering back to the days of scrounging for enough money to buy Kraft Macaroni 'n Cheese money in the couch, I finally said out loud, "I want a different life," and started controlling my pauper thoughts.
To become successful, I had to learn to master these two pauper thoughts:
"Wealthy people must be doing something wrong. It's so easy for them to make money, and so difficult for me."
Millionaires do what they love, they do it often, and they get better and better as a result. For instance, I have always loved

to be on stage, to perform, and to share with others what I learn. Am I good at performing because I enjoy it, or do I enjoy performing because I'm good at it? It doesn't matter, as long as the common denominator is enjoyment, and I follow what is in my heart and what makes me happy. Doing what you love, though, isn't always easy, and success is not a onetime achievement. I am constantly seeking more information and more knowledge to bring more value to my audience.

"Don't sell me anything. If you do, I'll lose."
Paupers are afraid to invest in their dreams. Millionaires know that the more cash flows, the more cash there is for everyone.

After 9/11, for once our political leaders delivered the right advice to a grieving American people: Our economy is in peril. If you want to help, go out and buy your kids the school clothes you were thinking of buying. Go out and buy that new car. Upgrade your home. Why? Because as long as money is flowing, our economy is sound. It's the same dynamic with your own personal economy. To increase financial awareness and abundance, plant seeds in places where they can grow. My good friend, the investor and best-selling author Robert Kiyosaki, says you should always invest in income-generating assets. Paupers hear that and say, "I'll only invest in real estate, because that shows an immediate return." That's not what Robert is saying.

An income-generating asset can be as wide as the universe. Let me give you an example.

One of my students, Jerry Arrola, had a water company that he sold at a great profit and then retired. Since his military service, he liked flying helicopters, so he bought one, quickly upgraded to another…and another…, until his wife told him to stop buying "toys"; he was wasting his money. Instead of getting rid of his copters, Jerry, who has a "millionaire mindset," told himself, "I'm going to have my toys make me money." He now owns the largest helicopter-training facility in the world headquartered in Nevada, with facilities in 15 states, Silver State Helicopters, generates over $100 million dollars a year in revenue. He bought what he wanted and turned it into an income-generating asset.

Millionaires think differently; we buy what we want and then figure out how to use that to make money, that's what I'm trying to impress upon you. Are you holding on too tightly to your current assets?

By increasing your ability to risk, you get more in return. The great hockey player Wayne Gretzky put it his way – You miss every shot you don't take.

Recently, I had the great fortune to dine with rebel billionaire Richard Branson, who founded Virgin Airlines. Faced with a decision to sell his beloved airline and walk away with half a billion dollars – he put it all back on the table and leveraged many billions more to start new businesses, including travel into outer space.
Ask yourself today, What would a millionaire do right now? Spend two hours arguing about a cell phone bill? Get stressed because they didn't get a decent raise? No! They would ask their boss, "How can I be in business with you?", or, better yet, ask, "How can I start or buy my own business?" It's time to unleash the millionaire in you.

Part 2 — Think Rich
How to Unleash Your "Inner" Prosperity

Learn Millionaire Habits
By Marshall Sylver

Real estate won't make you wealthy, the Internet doesn't print cash, and the stock market can't make you rich. <u>You</u> make you rich; more specifically, your habits make you rich. There's no way around it; your habits either make you or break you. You will have either discipline or regrets.

All happy, healthy and wealthy people develop, and master, five key personal habits:

1. Spiritual Health
2. Work-Life Balance
3. Priority management
4. Great Vision
5. Plan Setting

I emphasize "happy and healthy" for a reason. I wouldn't dream of teaching you how to make money without helping you to establish the proper foundation that allows you to enjoy your wealth. Learn and master these millionaire habits, and you'll be able to capitalize on the wealth-building vehicles described throughout this book. If you don't – you'll have regrets later, and wish you had!

Let's look at the first successful habit, and the true foundation of all wealth.

1. Spiritual Health

If you think being poor is tough, try being rich without being spiritually centered. Spiritual health is understanding that, ultimately, all of the money in the world isn't going to make you happy. If you don't like yourself when you're poor, you sure won't like yourself when you're rich – in fact, money makes the struggle harder.

That's why it's important to find a spiritual ideology that works for you. Finding wealth without finding peace is setting yourself up for disaster. Money can create paranoia, distance you from the people you love, and stimulate and create addictions. Wealth gives you enough money to indulge yourself with harmful things like drugs, alcohol, greed and worse. Instead, armed with a spiritual discipline, you'll be able to do the effective thing," and do it daily, so you can learn to truly love yourself and be freed up to do good work. "There really is no right or wrong, just consequences.

Spiritual health starts with the knowledge that the size of your bank account doesn't dictate your self worth. By truly liking who you are – with or without money – you'll make much better judgments and not get bogged down in emotional quicksand. In the course of building a successful business, it's normal to have setbacks. There will be bumps in the road, that is guaranteed. By being spiritually healthy, you'll be secure in your own identity and more willing to take calculated risks that are the foundation of creating wealth.

Spiritual health keeps you clear minded and joyful without worrying about the future. It also gives a strong moral foundation to enjoy your wealth. Ever wonder why the rich get richer? Because they have a spirit of gratitude; they're grateful for what they have. This spirit of gratitude allows them to look for what is working everyday. We always find what we are looking for. What we focus on expands. This mindset allows you to constantly deal with what emerges and find it not only useful, but actually perfect.

2. Work-Life Balance

I wouldn't dream of teaching you how to create wealth without teaching you how to create balance first.   Money without balance is the surest way down that slippery slope to a living hell.

You need to create and maintain mental, physical, relational, and then financial balance. When your priorities are in order, wealth will come easily and readily to you. You'll be happier and much more effective.

Notice the order I laid out: mental, physical, relational, and then financial. Most people reverse the order.
Balance begins with good mental health, otherwise the battle to create wealth is nearly impossible. Paying attention to your mental "diet" shapes your ability to succeed. Just like junk food that makes the body sluggish, feeding your mind "junk food" makes your mind sluggish, too. Millionaires and successful entrepreneurs pay close attention to what they read. Most read and study the biographies of people who have succeeded before

them, and avoid reading the newspaper everyday, since much of the news is sensationalized and filled with gossip. Focus your reading on content that is positive, uplifting, and teaches you something useful.

Since your thoughts create your emotions, taking control of your thoughts automatically allows you to respond rather than to react. Instead, your needs now become your desires; this allows you to do what's most effective, rather than to react because you feel your rights have been violated. Having rights set you up to be wronged. In the world of making money, often, you will be offended, since the other dogs are out looking for their feast as well. Surrender to the fact that business isn't fair. Once you accept that, you won't experience the emotional charge that you get from feeling like someone took advantage of you. You will simply learn the lesson and move on.

Balance means you understand that time spent with family, time spent contributing to your community, and time spent with your "higher power" are all essential to creating not only wealth, but satisfaction.

I travel a great deal, and realized that the most valuable asset I have is my time, not just as it relates to income-generating, but also because it cuts into the time I am able to spend maintaining the balance for which I strive. For these reasons, I gave up on commercial flying a long time ago. On any given trip, I spent three and a half hours to reach a commercial airport, rather than one of the 5,000 regional airports that are usually 15 minutes away from anybody's home. I had to park my car, get in line with hundreds, and even thousands, of other travelers, go through security, reach the gate, and then pray that my flight would be on time. Once I finally deplaned, I had to wait for my baggage, which was sometimes delayed by 45 to 60 minutes, before I was able to head toward my final destination – only to repeat this process on the way home. Seven extra hours each time I traveled!

By flying privately, I now drive seven minutes from my home to the nearest airport. I pull my car up to my jet, my pilot unloads the baggage from the trunk, and I get on board. My tray table is down on takeoff and landing, just because I can. I'm handed my favorite beverage, and I'm in the air and on my way to my destination within 15 minutes of leaving my home. When I land, I repeat the process. If I travel only twice a week, then I add 14 hours to my ability to maintain balance and increase productivity. Can you imagine how much more inspired you can be when you don't have to suffer the anxiety of commercial travel? Mastering this next habit helped me increase my Work-Life Balance.

3. Priority Management

If you're always working and not getting ahead, you're getting the wrong things done first. Millionaires tackle head on what I call the "Worst Things First List"; those tasks the ordinary person puts off that, ironically, most need to get done. Remember that millionaires earn $1,000,000 a year joyfully. Paupers (those earning less than $1,000,000 a year), are constantly busy doing busy things, but never accomplishing anything of value. Do not mistake action for accomplishment.
I teach students in my Millionaire Mentorship Program to control their priorities. Priority management teaches you to maintain balance in your life, so you don't jeopardize your

health or relationships. You cannot control or even manage time; you can only manage what is most important, which are your priorities. I tell my students to plan their entire day in advance for maximum productivity, to accomplish their most important priorities first. If they run out of time at the end of the day, the priorities that get put off are the ones of least importance.

Priority management is also the key that unlocks creative thinking that generates wealth. Contrary to what some think, creativity doesn't happen in a sudden burst of inspiration; it's a disciplined process that achieves results by focusing on a specific outcome.

Creative people, who become wealthy people, get more done in less time because they manage time in a planned, effective order. They focus their time on creating something new or innovative. I speak from my own experience. I do my best creative thinking after my workouts. My endorphin levels are high. My confidence is up, since I have just done something good for myself. Therefore, after working out in the morning, I schedule one hour to focus only on creativity. I turn off my cell phone, email and Instant Messaging programs, and tell anyone who interrupts that I'm focusing on a creative project and will get back to them in an hour.
Try this for 21 days, and see what happens.

4. Great Vision

Do what you love and the money will follow: Focus on being
the best at something and there will always be a market for your
goods and services.

This lesson will help you to see beyond the challenges and think
big. Small plans equal small motivations. People who create
wealth are just like you, with one exception – they have more
clarity of vision , and they're much more excited about their
future. Napoleon Hill, in his scholarly work, Think and Grow
Rich, defines purpose: Knowing what your final outcome is in
advance, seeing the successful completion of your objectives,
and being confident about its successful completion. By being
secure in what you're doing, and where you're going, the
inevitable trials and tribulations along the way become
manageable, and even exciting.

The theory of relativity wasn't created on a blackboard; it was
created when Albert Einstein imagined himself on the tip of a
beam of light traveling through space. Walt Disney created the
term "imagineering" to describe the building of his dreams. A
successful developer doesn't look at a piece of undeveloped
land and see dirt; he sees a beautiful building or development,
and people in a bidding war for the privilege of owning a piece.
Great vision is the ability to see things before they happen.
Millionaires almost always speak in the future tense. They
speak of the projects as if they are already completed, because
in their mind, they are. I call this process of projection,
"Entrepreneurial Exaggeration." The entrepreneur isn't lying,
but believe with all their heart and soul that what they set out to
accomplish is already done. They are only doing the very thing

that is the foundation of all great things, they are projecting forward. Show me someone who knows where he or she is going, and I promise you – everyone will want to come along!

5. Plan Setting

What's the difference between a person whose dreams remain just dreams and someone who gets things done? Planning. I teach people in my seminars to remove the word "goal" from their vocabulary. Since your subconscious computer (your mind) will only produce exactly what you tell it to, aiming for a goal is very different then executing a plan. You don't need to know every step to start. Whatever you envision right now, whatever you aspire to in this moment, you already have some of the elements in hand. Take the first step, and the next step will become clear.

Put your vision on paper. Grab a pen and piece of paper and describe your perfect working day, from the moment you wake up to the moment you go to sleep. With whom do you interact? Who is on your team? How much money do you make from your activities? What great fun do you have?
By doing that, you take the first step toward making that mental picture a reality. Once you do, you can start to "Chunk it Down" into doable steps.

Here are the basic element of Plan Setting:
Plan High. Small plans do not inspire. Big plans make you passionate. Most people are playing a small game, and produce small results. John D. Rockefeller said, "Play with pennies, you make pennies. Play with dollars; you make dollars." Worst case scenario: You accomplish only part of your plan. You wanted

to be a billionaire, and you only became a multimillionaire instead. Poor baby!

<u>Chunk it Down</u>. Small, bitesize steps. Even if it's not all doable right now, some is. A steady and certain march towards your plan will get you further than you realize. Critical mass takes over at some point, and all the things you have done suddenly add up. Looking at the big picture of anything can be overwhelming, so when you feel a task is too big, ask yourself this question. Post it near your workspace, so you can refer to it whenever you feel stuck:
"What is powerful, productive, positive, and leads me towards what I am working on? Do it now!"

<u>Action vs. production quotas</u>: In the beginning of any game, it's important to set yourself up to win. List what you will do, instead of what you will accomplish. Call 10 potential customers in one hour is an action quote; closing three new sales is a production quota. You don't need to lose 10 pounds, you need to get to the gym every day. The fat comes off when you take action. Taking consistent, powerful, productive action in the present moment will always move you closer to what you want.

<u>Personal Alterations.</u> What is stopping you from getting what you want? Who you are always determines what you get. Something about you, and something that you consistently do, has been stopping you from the living the life you deserve. What personal habit is standing in your way? Procrastination? Complacency? Pride? Ego? Take a personal inventory, and make a plan for change. If you can't figure this out, you are in denial. Truly effective millionaires and billionaires can easily

tell you what they need to change to make themselves more effective. It's called self-awareness. Be self-aware, and every change becomes obvious.

Read Your Plan Every Day. Make it an obsession. Post pictures, drawings, and reminders everywhere you turn, so you become what you plan: successful. Taste it, see it, feel it. Let it become your reality before the world even thinks it is a possibility. Start "Acting As If" it is already true, and you will attract the people you need to accomplish it.

Millionaires and billionaires are constantly feeding their minds with healthy information. Like any muscle, the mind needs to exercise or it will die. Reading is one way to stimulate your mind "muscle," because it requires you to be active instead of passive. Reading everyday also can improve the way you communicate. Not only will your vocabulary increase, but you will read the biographies about how other successful people became wealthy due in part to their ability to communicate. Great businesspeople like Richard Branson or Mark Cuban, or any other millionaires or billionaires, are also great communicators. The wealthiest man on the planet, Bill Gates, is the wealthiest because of his incredible ability to communicate his ideas, his creativity, and his motivation to other people to inspire them to be more than they thought they could be. Communication equals wealth. The quality of our lives is the quality of our communication, both with ourselves and with outside world.   I see communication with ourselves as programming. It's the 1,500 words per minute whizzing through our brain that tell us who we are, or are not; what we can be, or not be; what we can do, or not do; and what we can have, or not have. Communication with the outside world is called influence. Influence is not the ability to get somebody else to say "'yes" to what you are offering. True influence is the ability to persuade somebody else to ask for what you are selling and have them believe it was their idea.

I have made millions of dollars by helping others get what they want. The challenge is, Most people don't know what they want until you tell them. I call the process of influencing other people to ask for what you are selling the "Persuasion Equation."

There are five steps:

1. Gain rapport and trust. We don't buy anything at any price from someone we don't trust.

2. Elicit the buyer's outcome. Your job as a master influencer is to make what you are selling look like what the other person wants.

3. Give the buyer a directive to take the action steps necessary to get what they want. Other people need permission, and seek validation, to take the actions that will get them what they seek.

4. If they resist, give more information. The only reason a person says no to a directive is that they fear a loss. Influence is playing with the buyer's resistance, and knowing that is all part of the process. On average, people say no five time before they say yes.

5. Give the directive to take action again.

Repeat Steps 4 and 5 until you reach your outcome of influencing the other party.

Being an effective communicator both internally and externally requires practice. It is a learned skill set, and does not happen naturally. For more information, I suggest you read the best book ever written on the subject, Passion, Profit and Power

(Simon & Schuster, 1995). It was a glorious day for fools when modesty became a virtue, don't you agree?

 Right now you're faced with the decision to move ahead, or stay stuck where you are.   In the movie, The Shawshank Redemption, Andy Duphrea says, "Get busy living or get busy dying." So what are you gonna do? Make a commitment today to apply and master the habits of wealthy people described in this chapter, and you'll be ready to use the wealthbuilding strategies my colleagues share throughout this book.

The truth is, You've never been comfortable being a pauper; it's not your natural state. You're a millionaire. The money may not have been deposited in your bank account, but it's still who you are. Don't wait for the world's validation; know it is your soul. Whether it's a better car, house, or lifestyle, a life once expanded never contracts. Once you get accustomed to living in a more effective, more powerful and passionate way, I promise, you'll never go back to your old life. In fact, you'll smile and ask, "What took me so long?"

Here's to looking out the window of my private jet, and seeing you wave back through the window of yours.

("A Wallet Once Expanded," by Marshall Sylver. Copyright pending. Used with permission. Any other use, please contact sylver.com.)

Swami Ramananda Maharaj

If you think wealth and spirituality don't mix, meet Swami Ramananda Maharaj. He lives down the street from me. He knows the richest people in the world, personally and literally. He is flown in private jets by London royalty, and is spiritual consultant to some of the most powerful people on the planet. He is showered with money, but in the true fashion of a Swami, he passes it on to help orphans in India and others in need.

I asked him to share his insight. The following are his words.

"When I work with people like Elton John, Cher, Bette Midler at the tranquility center at Caesar's Palace where I'm the director, I'm constantly speaking with people about making their lives sustainable. I think when you look at wealth from our perspective, you really have to embrace this idea, that everything that flows into us is a Goddess and she needs to be respected. When you look at it from that perspective, it changes the way you handle money, it changes the way you look at prosperity, and you start to look at your life from the standpoint of sustainability. I think this is the reason why the Hindu tradition embraces this concept- that it's o.k. to be prosperous, it's really o.k. to be sustainable.

Many people are coming to me asking how they can improve their lives, how they can bring prosperity into their lives, how they can make a more sustainable situation in life for themselves. First we start with the mind, with yoga, with meditation, with a more positive mental attitude. As you wake up every day, don't turn on CNN, do not go on Facebook, and do not run to Starbucks. The first thing you do is stretching, you start breathing, and you put yourself in a positive mental state to be receptive. When you are receptive, then you can ask for the prosperity. You can treat your house with the Feng Shui to create the prosperity. You know, I've taken a lot of people that've really hit the skids. Some people lost their wealth just completely, and we start over again… we start looking at where they live, we start looking at their lifestyle, I start looking at their mental attitude, and everything starts to change, so it's wonderful for me to see these successes. I knew some people who's companies were going to bottom out, and we made the changes and brought in the positive energy, and then those people reported back to me they made 25 million in two weeks, …to them it's like a miracle.

These people are creating a tremendous amount of wealth, and the wealth is being used for hospitals, orphanages, and for the education to bring up whole groups of people, so it's very very important to teach people how to use that energy, the prana, the life-force. I'm very excited, because this is the way that I feel that I can work with people and share all of these years of knowledge and study and information … India, China, Thailand, Sri Lanka, around the world … I've spent these last fifty something years just absolutely being on the road and learning from every great master that would unveil themselves to me. It's about making our lives more rich, more sustainable, and more spiritual- you know, to take your wealth and spiritualize your wealth, to take your health and spiritualize your health.

When you get to know some of the people you really see at the top, the ultra-rich …I've worked with them on charitable programs. I sit on the board of directors of a lot of different charities from schools for blind children, schools for deaf. In India alone, I have over 1200 orphans I'm working with on a daily basis, and these (wealthy) people are the people that come in and help me. Their heart understands what I'm trying to do, and they feel they have the money and that money has been given to them by God to do good things, so I think this idea that all wealthy people are bad, or that all wealthy people are selfish is kind of ludicrous, because if you really believe that way, there would be no money for our great charities, there would be no scholarship programs. These things are all coming from the wealthy. Many of our halls that are built for public places to gather, like the symphony, the opera, the ballet, …all built for our enrichment. So you have to look at wealth as opportunity. The opportunity is suddenly given to you to do all the things that you might have dreamed of in your life, and not just for yourself but for your family and for others. Prosperity is the opportunity and the strength and confidence that you can manifest the money to be everything that you want to be. For prosperity to come into your home, she has to be invited, everything has to be right in your house in terms of Feng Shui (the Vastu), and your attitude has to be right.

These prosperous, wealthy CEOs, the heads of these organizations, they know this is all about energy and how you keep the energy positive.

There was a prayer I once prayed when I was in India. I was in a monastery, I shaved my head in the initial stages of becoming who I am today. I remember, I got on my knees and I said to

God "Everything that I am, and everything that I have … is for you, for your Earth use." And the minute I prayed that prayer, money came to me in waterfalls of abundance. I was a millionaire by the time I was 35, and I saw that as a golden opportunity to get out and to give and to give and to give. When you leave this world, what is in your spiritual bank account? Your spiritual bank account is everything that you have given… but you can't give anything if you don't have anything, so you've got to welcome the sustainability and the abundance into your life so that you can make a difference in this world. That is the big key to me to living a healthy, successful, happy, rich fulfilled life here on Earth.

We're all just trustees for the wealth. Do we really own anything in this world? We come in naked, and we're going to leave naked. You can't take it with you. Look at the great Egyptian Pharaohs and all the gold they were buried with. None of that is there anymore, it all got taken. There is no way you can hang on to anything in this world. But to let it pass through you and to be a good steward of everything that's given to you while you've got it… that's the key to make a difference.

You have to make a difference in your own life before you can make a difference in the lives of others. So it's very important that you take good care of yourself. You don't have to practice some form of self-denial. I think the important thing is to welcome the wealth in. Do something great for yourself and your family, and do something great for others. You know, that's the true balance of living. Namaste."

Swami Ramananda Maharaj   http://www.swamiramananda.com
Author of "Bliss Now" and "From India with Love"

Richard Helfrich

When I met Richard back in 1989, he was running a motion picture company and had spent the last five years rebuilding his heart trying to avoid a heart transplant. He owned mansions in Hollywood, Hawaii, Palm Springs and probably a couple more I didn't know about. When he left the house, he had to decide whether to take the Rolls, the Mercedes, the Porsche or the Ferrari. Yet despite all that, he is deeply spiritual and respectful of all life. Like me, his quest for truth and real health led to leaving Hollywood and simplifying his life for what really mattered. He is now health consultant to some of the most famous people imaginable. We've been great friends for almost 25 years now and when I asked him to share his secrets in this book, he was on a plane to Argentina. He emailed the following text.

"Studying medicine became my passion and my love, and shortly after meeting Markus decided to leave entertainment and focus on natural medicine full time. Having spent the last 10 years working in the business on all of Steven Spielberg's movies and many others, it was a leap of faith to see if a career could be forged from what I had learned trying to save my own life.

Having been successful in entertainment, I had for years given advice when asked that success came from putting one foot in front of the other and aiming for a goal not fixated on how you were going to get there. I was applying that advice to myself and not caring if I made a dime because now I was only going to do what I loved.

Relying on the famous Admiral Byrd quote when asked how he set about being the first to explore Antarctica;

"That only when he committed himself did all the material resources he never could have imagined materialize".

So I started taking on whatever came at me, cancer, viruses, autoimmune diseases, etc. My attitude was let's figure it out and after rebuilding my own heart felt there was nothing the body could not heal, there was no self-destruct button in the body. I was very fortunate to have a lot of people trust me with their health and over the years witnessed many success stories from so many who had the courage to fight for their life and not be a victim thinking their disease was a drug deficiency.

Having also had the privilege to work with people like Princess Diana who encouraged me to write my first book and helped get it published opening the door to writing three more on everything from how the body works to what it takes to have a functioning immune system. I have worked with many celebrities, captains of industry and other famous people ...there is one trait that I have always looked for in choosing to work with someone - do they have the courage to fight for their life and the discipline to see it through. Being able to work with people around the globe, travel and experience first hand the growing consciousness people have about taking control of their health and not willing to be medicated into submission has been truly exciting. This is the moment- the entry point. I have never hesitated in my life because I never thought I could not achieve whatever the goal if I was willing to give 100%."
Richard Helfrich

Markus Rothkranz

Hi again! I'm back. Did you see common traits in those three? I sure hope so. And I hope you are starting to get some courage now to step outside your comfort zone and finally start doing what you are here to do! All you need to do is commit 100% to YOU and your heart. No fear. Learn from mistakes, they are your gifts. Help others and learn to give. Don't fear losing anything because nothing is yours anyway.

Money and wealth is not yours to own. It is entrusted to you by the universe to do great things with. The instructions of what to do with it is encoded into your cells in the form of yearning. It is the voice speaking to you from inside your heart, not your head. As soon as you start listening to it and have the strength and courage to follow it, the Universe will give you all the resources and power you need to do what you are here to do.

You are put here for a reason.

The moment you surrender yourself to your higher purpose, is the moment your true life starts. A new door opens, welcoming you to...

THE NEW WORLD

We are entering a new era of consciousness.

All living things deserve happiness.

Right now the world is imbalanced and all the other species on the planet are suffering because one particular species- man- is afraid. So afraid in fact, that it protects itself with barriers. It wants security, so it accumulates all kinds of unnatural stuff to hide in and surround itself with. It covers its body with clothing and makeup, then surrounds that with a big dwelling, then protects that with gates, walls, locks, weapons, a security system and an insurance policy. It hides and protects its true thoughts and feelings, even from its own mate. It goes so far as to even hide its true feelings from itself.

Why? What is it hiding from ? What is it trying to protect itself from?

The ironic answer is found in the scariest movies. What we are most afraid of... is already inside the house... as a matter of fact... it's INSIDE OF US !

What we are most afraid of... is the truth... that maybe we are not good enough, so we spend our entire lives trying to validate our worth to others, to prove we are good enough.

Good enough for what?

As a child we look up to our parents. We try to win their approval. They gave us life. We want to prove our worthiness for being alive. We do not want to be a waste of space and resources.

We have the bodies of adults now, but our consciousness is still that of a child, trying to win approval of others... still trying to prove we are not just a waste of space and resources. We see the clock ticking... the years going by and we feel the pressure to make something of ourselves or else be written off as failures (or so we think). Nobody wants to be a failure. We want to feel we are worth something ...that we contributed to the big game of life somehow. That we left our mark. We want respect. Those who enslave others have a desperate need for respect and try to force it. This deep need we have to exist for a reason, and be acknowledged for it, is a profoundly embedded human trait. Animals just exist. Humans need to exist for a reason. Our consciousness is our gift and our burden.

For hundreds of thousands of years, this consciousness has been a mystery and the greatest minds have tried to make sense of it. We are only now starting to realize the scope or what we have in our possession. Until now, it has been an immature child controlling our lives and everything around us, in fact, it has brought this world to the brink of extinction. Until now, the human mind has had no real focus, and as a result of this imbalance, over 95% of the human race is in poverty and enslaved in confusion and fear. The other 5% have a lot of power and wealth but don't really have a clue what to do with it. Meanwhile, the rest of the natural world is trying to desperately hang on waiting for us to get our act together. The animals and plants are all being poisoned while we sit here worrying about our petty bills.

Something has to change. And it is.

Like the greatest movie ever made, it's finally dawning on us that the answer to our problems has been inside us all along. And what's even more spine chilling... is that the source of our problems (the human mind with all its insecurities)... is also the very thing that's going to save us and turn everything around.

We are just starting to realize that we carry within us the greatest gift in the universe. God created his masterpiece in us and has been sitting back smiling, waiting for this moment. We have inside the most powerful force in the universe- the power to create anything. God gave us the ultimate gift. Our minds can literally create any reality we want, and we haven't even been using one millionth of its power. This seed was planted a long, long time ago, and it's just now starting to wake up. The time has come. The awakening has started.

The ugly caterpillar that has been ravaging all the leaves (damaging the environment) is cocooning itself and imploding (economy collapse), its body used as a food source (inner restructuring) by a new life form that will break open the old hard shell (the old protective barriers of insecurity and fear we have built around ourselves), and emerge into the light as a new life form...(butterfly)... a life form of beauty and color... one that is no longer confined to crawling and eating leaves. This new life form sips the nectar of flowers and has the ability to fly on the wings of sheer beauty wherever it wants from one flower to the next. This is the analogy of true prosperity. You are here at the greatest moment of human history my friends. The great awakening. And inside you right now is the key- the most powerful force in the universe.

One by one, all over the world, we are feeling the urge to be reborn. We are shedding the old to make way for the new. Old heavy things are being taken away if we want it or not. We are becoming lighter. Our consciousness is universally rising in frequency... the entire world is moving from fear to courage. As the frequency rises, our frustration and anger is transformed into forgiveness and love, and as a result, we are finally given the prosperity we have known is our birthright from the beginning. We are not here anymore to crawl and destroy ...we are here to fly and be beautiful.

As you change, the whole world changes. However you want the world to be, become it yourself first. By empowering yourself, you empower others, setting a magic chain reaction into play that transforms the entire world. There is enough magic, beauty and prosperity to go around for everyone. Do not fear lack. The entire world and everyone in it deserves happiness.

I am not suggesting everyone in the world be in a mansion. Most don't need that or want it. I know rich people that gave it all up to go live in a grass hut in Fiji and live off coconuts. There are millions of people on the verge of starvation while people in America live in beautiful suburban homes driving huge vehicles and do nothing but complain. If those starving people could rise just a few notches to where they had decent water, food and a roof, that to them would be what a mansion is to us. It's all relative. This is important- just because there are starving people does not mean you shouldn't be prosperous and living a good life, otherwise read this book again. Poor people waste more money than rich people because most of what rich people own is an investment, not a consumable that loses its value the minute you buy it. The more power you have, the more good you can do with it. And what is the source of that power? Right- your heart! If your heart needs a fancy car to feel good, then fine, go get one- if that's what it takes to power you up so you can help millions overseas. Never look at the negative- always look at the positive- that's the ONLY way the new world will work. Stop with all the negativity, jealousy and ill feelings. They only bring the same back to you. Wish others the greatest success and you will get the same in return.

I remember when I was down, I would go to airports and get a rush from the power of the jets. I would fill my cells with the energy of their mighty force and their ability to soar above the clouds to anywhere in the world. I went to the terminal and absorbed the energy of all the people being reunited and the happiness they felt. My house in Vegas is right in the flight path of the private jets. Every time one roars over my house, I cheer them on. They excite me. It's like Tom Cruise in the movie Top Gun, speeding alongside the runway on his motorcycle as the fighter jets take off and cheering them on. I knew one day I would be flying in those jets and I did. It powered me up and made me feel like anything was possible. This power gave me the strength and inspiration to start healing the world. As long as you use the gifts of this world for good, you are on the right path. Get this through your head-

IT'S OK TO CELEBRATE LIFE !!!

We have a monumental amount of difference to make in a short amount of time, so lighten your load, pack your bags and get out there in the world, today! No more excuses.

Right now we are using paper money... that may change next month, it doesn't matter. Whatever is used as currency will eventually be used fairly because the only thing that lasts is truth. Everything else falls away. It is the law of nature. Only truth can survive ...and the greatest expression of truth is love. Wish everyone well, no matter who they are, and the Universe will repay you handsomely.

Your mind and heart are the ultimate internet connection- it is directly connected with the source of all creation. You cannot lie, cheat or hide the truth anymore because of this connection. Whatever you feel, will instantly be felt and heard by everyone around you, so what you put out will come right back to you instantly. So focus all your energy on being the very best you can be. Get rid of anything holding you back, so you can fly. Give like you've never given before. Rise above all resistance and fear to become the most prosperous YOU possible that inspires and helps others, and in return, you will be given the greatest kingdom to live in you could ever imagine. Whatever you think prosperity is, it's nothing compared to where you will end up shortly. Let go. Be the most honorable person you can. Start with the person right next to you right now. Surprise them with an amazing gift of grace. Then move on to the next. Show the Universe you are a new person, one who is serious about making a difference. No more negative thoughts because your mission is too important.

The world needs as many people as possible to rise in frequency, prosper and shine. By rising, you pull others up with you. No more letting yourself be pulled down to other people's level- it's time they rise to yours.

So rise and be prosperous. It is your duty !

The world needs your light. Light it up baby.

The only limit to our realization of tomorrow will be our doubts of today. Franklin D. Roosevelt

Success is...

Success is not a formula. It's not a thing. It's WHO you are. Stop going after the money. Work on <u>you</u>. You must know who you are and be willing to stand up for what you are here to do. Every successful person in the world found the strength to be themselves despite what everyone else told them. Remember, all the resistance you are getting is just a test to see if your are strong enough to handle the riches waiting for you. This whole world around you is just a test. Forget what the economy is doing. The richest people in the world became rich during hard times. I will keep repeating that. A master is someone who can take something that seems negative and turn it into something positive, and the only thing stopping you from doing that is disbelief, doubt and fear. You already have everything you need right now to start being successful. I was naked in the desert with nothing, and within a month was driving a Ferrari. All you need is to feel the fire inside you like Rocky, hear the theme song playing in your heart, get up at 5 in the morning and start running. There is a champion inside you waiting to burst out. Its been chained up way too long. It's high time you claimed your space in the world. Let us know who you are. Make us proud. Start right now. Step outside your comfort zone into the spotlight. The entire Universe is watching and ready to back you up as long as you prove you have the guts to be strong and commit all or nothing. Right now.

Show the world who you are.   Right Now.

If there's a will, prosperity can't be far behind.

W.C. Fields

WELCOME TO THE NEW YOU !

You can't just rant and cry and proclaim what you want.
Something inside you needs to accept that it's UP TO YOU to
get it done. You need to tell yourself you've had it with waiting
for others. You need to look at the situation like NO ONE else
is going to come through for you. They are all caught up in
their own dramas. The only one who's going to come through
for you is YOU. Stop waiting. No one really knows how to do
it as well as you anyway. Its never been done before the way
you are going to do it. So draw up the plans and start doing it!
You are Noah. Build the Ark. Show everyone you can do it.
Grab some paper and draw the plans. Figure out every detail.
Let it obsess you. This is not a hobby, it's the reason you are
here. Stop living for others and start doing what you are here
for. The world needs people like you for inspiration. Set the
example. A revolution starts with one person taking a step
forward against all others.

And guess what. That's all it takes. When people see you take
that step, it will give them goose bumps. Some will join you.
Suddenly you have help. If you listen to your true calling and
take that step, and stay true with total integrity... the entire
universe will get behind you and you will change the world.
The universe just wants to see you take that first step. It wants
to see you are serious. It wants to see you are committed. The

moment you have had it with the way things have been and can't stand one more minute and say "this is it. It all changes here and now. Watch out world, I have been activated"... that's the moment everything changes. You can feel it. Nothing is the same again. It's like you've suddenly been transported into another dimension with different energy. The actors look the same, but the movie is different.

Welcome to the world of Quantum reality.

You just zapped yourself into another movie, and this time you are the hero, not the victim. You are in charge of everything. Power and electricity crackles from your fingertips and fire shoots from your eyes. Everyone is waiting for your commands. Whatever you want is now manifested. To others it may seem like magic. They smile and celebrate you. They want what you have. You are their inspiration, their strength, their light, and you don't have to drain your energies anymore for them. All you have to do is be you. That's what they want and need. That's what the universe wants and needs. You are designed for a reason- a very special purpose. Your job is to inspire everything around you with positive energy. The way you do this is to simply be yourself and follow your dreams and make them happen. Your job is not to follow someone else's dream. Your job is to stay true to YOU. Maybe that means joining forces with someone or something else, that's fine, as long as you are doing what you are designed for. It could be just being a great plumber. Every team member has a special task. And good ones are priceless. It's what makes teams win world championships. But this isn't a contest. It's a healing fest.

The world needs you. And every moment you wait- every second you hold back, you are denying the world your special gift. You are a race horse, a space shuttle, a fighter jet, fully fueled and ready to burst out full throttle and save the world.

Stop with the mediocrity. Don't embarrass the universe. Claim your space on the throne. You are royalty. Start demanding your rights. Claim your power right now because people all over the world are lost and dying. They need guidance and direction. Take action. Make the universe proud.

Don't waste one more second.

It all changes right now.

By the time you read the next sentence in this book, everything everywhere will have changed.

Every thought you have changes everything everywhere. Make it count.

Love and Light

Your imagination is your preview of life's coming attractions"

Albert Einstein.

Even the tiniest thought is a seed that can change the world

Markus

For more books, DVDs and life-changing products by Markus, go to **MarkusProducts.com**

The Free Markus Newsletter is at
MarkusNews.com